Be Aware, Be Faithful or Be @ Risk

Gordon Brown, PhD

ISBN 978-1-64559-184-9 (Paperback)
ISBN 978-1-64559-185-6 (Digital)

Covenant Books, Inc.
11661 Hwy 707
Murrells Inlet, SC 29576
www.covenantbooks.com

What Is Happening to My World and Me?

Everyone wonders about the world around us and our part in it. Some wonder more than others. Some wander more than others. Each of us struggle with outside influences that we cannot control as well as inside influences that we should control. We seek new ways to control those influences but often find that we cannot or choose not to meet them head on. We then make life easy or hard or both and reap what we sow.

Life is about living which is an accumulation of personal successes and failures. And yet, each life is an integral part of God's creation. We are called to be His instruments midst a sinful world, one that is sometimes quiet; oftentimes, noisy and always unpredictable. We are called to create a melody that survives in both easy and hard times, a song that can be enjoyed in the quiet and heard over the noise. To accomplish our calling, we must be acutely aware of ourselves, interpersonal situations, the economics of life, and influential powers in the world. The better aware we are of all that is fixed and all that moves in our lives, the better we can respond to spiritual, economic, and political situations. The better aware we are of the way things work and are trending, the better we can respond to immediate and future opportunities and threats.

Life and the economics of life run in cycles. While the quiet and the noise continue to ebb and flow, God plays a creational melody. The more aware we are of those cycles outside us and in us, the better able we are to play our best part in His creation. God calls us to be instruments of peace, of light, of salt, and of leaven. He has designed us to prosper and placed us in situations where we can make a difference. Unfortunately, we often wallow in blindness.

There are times when blindness produces blindness. We see what we want to see. We act to maintain what we want to see, not what God would want for us. The times in which we now live are evidence of past and present blindness. The world has evolution and

3

revolution on its mind. Powers of the world think and act as if they are more potent than God.

This is a book about potency. It is about using your God-given powers of intellect, awareness, insight, and determination to change your world. You are the author of how you write your life's story. First, you must be aware that you are the author. Helping you be a little more aware of the economics of your life, the decisions you make, the friends you keep, the herds you follow, the values you embrace, the questions you ask, the wisdom you seek, the efforts you give, the prayers you pray, the battles you choose, and the clarity you should provide to yourself and others is what this book is about. It is intended to be an author's guide to help you write your best story possible. Once you see personal and corporate situations for what they are and what they can or will be, you will be a force for good and a willing instrument for God. Know that you are the prequel to the stories of situations and people you touch.

Prepare to read a book that will prepare you to make a positive impact. As you will see, there is a loose organization of the concepts presented in this book; however, what enters your mind and heart and what sticks long enough to make an impact on you and others is up to you and God.

The Economics of Life with God at the Helm

Life is a collection of situations. Our participation levels in one moment define the next moments and the moments after that. We succeed or fail by the choices we make, informed or uniformed, and the choices and reactions that others make. Economics (spiritual, personal, and corporate) influence those choices which, in turn, determine outcomes. Outcomes then take us to other choices which determine subsequent outcomes and the cycle progression continues.

We live "situational economics" each day in what we spend, how we work, how we invest, in whom we invest, what drives us, and how we relate to God. Production and consumption, investment and disinvestment, giving and taking are part of each life. Our intent is what drives us to act and to react. Little is uniform or perceived equally by all as the macro and microeconomics influences in our lives shape our ongoing motivations and actions or, at least, add to what we once knew and lived. The economics of life are much more than dollars and cents.

It is humanly impossible to comprehend all the factors that influence our decisions or how our decisions affect others or how the decisions of others affect us. Absolute best choices are hard to find in anything. We face uncertain, often tenuous, situations. We may have limited options from which to choose. Our presuppositions and perceptions of gain and loss lead us down decision paths with carrots and sticks lining the way. While each of us has a hand in making our personal and corporate economics for better or for worse, our part in it may be overstated. Behind the scenes, God's *Invisible Hand* is at work in us and through us, whether we see His hand or want His hand or not.

The difficulty we have in becoming situationally aware lies in our inability to comprehend the proximate elements of time, space, material, and persons and their proximate effects on each other. We have even greater difficulty in projecting the effects of the proximate on remote elements of time, space, material, and persons and vice versa. The remote can be as influential on the proximate as the proximate is on the remote. We are destined to make choices every day that produce ramifications for people who are affected by the time, space, and materiality of those choices. The economics of life always depend on an awareness level and ensuing choices for more than our material existences. We look for that one cause-and-effect relationship that can spur success, but productivity, wealth, and spiritual growth are objectives that never end and are often unmeasurable. Understanding the spiritual elements that face us and motivate us is a lifelong adventure.

God's *Invisible Hand* is a wild card when it comes to perceptions and outcomes because His works are beyond our understanding and expectations. There may be a sense of His presence, sometimes causing awe, and the greater our awareness of that presence, the more likely we are to incorporate Him into our thought process and, ultimately, our actions. We are indeed instruments of God's purposes; however, His purposes in the proximate and for the remote transcend our intents, understandings, and choices, which is why He is God.

Webster's New World Collegiate Dictionary (4th Edition) defines God as "any of various beings conceived of as supernatural, immortal, and having special powers over the lives and affairs of people," ascribing the potential for original creation of both the material and the spiritual realms to God. Implicit in that definition is the real possibility that such a creator is the ruler of the universe. The Christian view maintains that God is omnipotent, omnipresent, and omniscient at the same time and for all of time. Secular and humanistic views of God believe that God or gods exercise much less insight, power, and control of economic and spiritual matters of this world and the individual lives residing in the world than believers believe. Humanism contends that religion (and nonreligion), economics (including hunger), and physical health (including psychoses) are determining motivators while God, if there is a god for them, is benign and simply resides in the background.

The conflict between the Christian definition and others comes down to the creator/controller question of, "Who is in control of life, man or God?" If the answer is God, then, logically, a living God would not be passive with His creation, just as men are not passive in the production, consumption, and investment in their creations. Because man rarely sees with his eyes all that God does invisibly in the moment (and for future moments), the overarching importance of His invisible hand in both His economy and man's economy escapes most in most situations.

The more aware a mind, the more it recognizes that a forceful, yet often gentle, *Invisible Hand* influences each choice, each action, and each resulting action, producing both intended and unintended consequences. Free choice gets the ball rolling because free choice is at the center of both man's material economy and God's spiritual economy. The hand generates the pursuit of "betterment" of self and more than self, whether we are situationally aware or not, in time or for a future time.

Every choice we make is a value judgement. An asset may be chosen as valuable or risk may be avoided as more valuable. Personal values may conflict with corporate values, creating hard choices. Value judgments are often made absent in complete information or awareness of multiple options or likely consequences. Differing perceptions of reality produce different choices in minds and hearts. Critical value always rises to the top when needs are greatest.

In man's linear world, there are no perfect choices because there are no perfect standards. Man does not grasp the nonlinear dimensions of "perfect" or "complete." Perfect standards and measuring sticks can be found in the Bible; however, perfect responses to every occasion may not be recognized or translated because the storied characters of the Bible made choices under differing circumstances. But our awareness of the characters' situations, the characters' joys and sorrows, their trials and tribulations, and their faith and fainting lead to lessons learned for use in a proximate situation at hand.

A repeated need for God has existed throughout history. God's timing knows the best consequences to be derived from a situation and the actors and actions necessary to create the greatest value for His purposes. He knows the best choices and outcomes for the proximate situational moment and the remote consequences and moments moving forward.

Change is unpredictable in full because man's nature keeps things interesting. Man seeks "new" when "new" is better or cheaper. Better is best when more is offered for less in economic terms, but men and women can become so preoccupied with their own rewards while the spiritual, economic, and social and spiritual consequences, radiating outward and onward in the lives of others, go unnoticed until they must be. Successes and failures often then appear in unexpected ways. Since learning does not always come easily or endure, men and women show a propensity to repeat mistakes time and again and incur consequences accordingly.

One big mistake is thinking and accepting that others, including governments, can and should control and prosper one or many men's and women's economics. Governments can indeed both incentivize and constrain a man's choices; however, governments rarely promote an environment of "best economics" because too many in power fear change and fail to see the timely need for change. Political and economic power has a unique way of obscuring the fact that God is the author of change. Governments are of men not of the spirit.

Adam Smith's Invisible Hand at Work in the Economics of Our Lives

The *Invisible Hand* term has been used by Adam Smith and others to describe that force by which individual actions create unintended social and economic benefits for more than the actor. The Bible goes deeper, using the term "logos" to describe the spiritual force who created and has influenced the lives of men since the beginning of time. The Greeks thought it an impersonal force. The Hebrews maintained that the *Invisible Hand* is very personal for each of us.

Personal interactions form life as we know it. Personal exchanges among us are most efficient and rewarding when they benefit the most, the most. Men and women do not always need to sacrifice themselves fully to create the most for many. The *Invisible Hand* may direct us to achieve the maximum benefit for most according to God's good purpose, stepping into the human void. Some might call it social engineering from on high, however, that would eliminate free choice and free markets. The *Invisible Hand* permits free choice in context, one where the usefulness one person provides to another moves the needle forward. The pursuit of economic and spiritual profit (however defined) in rational self-interest ends up being best for many and, oftentimes, most.

Some argue that Adam Smith's *Invisible Hand* theory is used to justify *laissez-faire* economics (man should be free to accomplish most with least governmental controls) and capitalism itself. His critics have also suggested that the pursuit of self-interest in a free economy ends in selfishness which begets corruption, and the poor do not get a fair share. Critics of the critics maintain that too much fettering of an economy and individual choices result in inefficiency and, ultimately, the taking from the common man by the elites for equally corrupt purposes. Control is the bottom-line objective for those who have it and those who want it and for good or evil reasons.

Governments may attempt to channel self-interest in socially desirable ways, however, focus on the proximate does not adequately improve the lot of remote persons or timing. Not surprisingly, those who lust for control do not recognize the ultimate control of God. They do not comprehend that an overarching economy of God exists. They certainly do not comprehend the power of the Holy Spirit freely at work in both proximate and remote situations for the betterment of both the economy of man and the economy of God.

Is the *Invisible Hand* the Holy Spirit? It could be but only in part. The Holy Spirit is so much more. The Holy Spirit convicts of sin (John 16:7-8), abides (John 14:16-17), teaches and reminds us (John 14:26), guides to truth (John 16:13), empowers (Acts 1:8), bears fruit in us and through us (Galatians 5:22-23), advantages (John 16:7), and equips with varieties of spiritual gifts (1 Corinthians 12:4-7). The Holy Spirit is a strength in weakness, an advocate, a wise teacher, a prayer director, and a power on earth that touches hearts beyond what the eyes can see, and the ears can hear. The Holy Spirit uses both self-interest and selflessness for the Lord's purposes. That power and that purpose is far beyond the productive efficiencies theoretically provided to man's society by Adam Smith's economic *Invisible Hand*.

In daily practice, more tangible and intangible value is created when many possess complete freedom to act in the most efficient way, not at the beckon call of a powerful few and not at the hand of single misdirected soul. The greatest value is created when the Holy Spirit is permitted to indwell a soul, guiding that soul to work, to consider the needs of others, and to use rational self-interest to improve the economics of man and for God.

Two Economies in One

As mentioned, we live in *man's material economy and God's spiritual economy* concurrently, yet often fail to see their joint and their separate influences on us. We may succeed in the material and yet fail in the spiritual. When we focus solely on ourselves and our personal economics, we neglect to see that real success lies in making ourselves valuable to others, both materially and spiritually. Man's version of *Economics 101* is far different from God's in that our focus rests primarily on the material. God's economy includes the material but uses one soul or collective souls to overcome the constraints and restraints of the physical world.

Fundamentally, economics is a social science involving the production, distribution, investment and consumption of wealth. It includes related issues of labor, finance, freedom, taxation, and other positive and negative human creations. A lack of profits in spiritual and in money terms speak for themselves. A lack of production and wealth becomes visible when internal or external personal or economic variables—whether seen or not, measured or not, anticipated or not, friendly or not, or positive or not—result in challenges that force new directions.

A human scoreboard registers material gains and losses in our material moments but, generally, fails to account for work of the *Invisible Hand*. Hindsight is a great teacher, but man's inability to comprehend progressions behind the scenes limits his accounting. Material values fluctuate, and sustainability is given little attention until it becomes an issue. The human scoreboard often fails to recognize the fleeting nature of present and future values. Proximate values give way to remote creations with sustainability being the deciding factor.

The mathematical science for measuring affecting and affected variables is virtually impossible. Sophisticated econometric computer models are used to predict macro trends and public policy effects, using statistics and past trends as benchmarks. Short-term predictions can be somewhat accurate within linear limits. Volatility is, however, an inherent part of man's existence. The winds that buffet man's circumstances, expectations, temptations, subjugations, freedoms, loves, yearnings, investments, profits, and losses are never standard nor consistent. Standards set for God's economy, in contrast, are consistent by design.

Behavioral Economics and the Invisible Hand

If behavior begets economics and, at the same time, economics begets behavior, the attitudes and causes in which we invest alter the attitudes and causes of others who then change in similar or dissimilar fashion. The more people interact, the greater the multiplications. Profits and morality may multiply just like losses and immorality may multiply. External forces can either enhance the multiplication process or destroy it. The cycle of history attests to man's inevitable "going back to the future," often apart from God, continuing until reality convinces us of the need for God.

The study of *behavioral economics* is more an art than a science currently. That people act in self-interest is known, but a single utility or differing perceptions of utility in the moment and over time is hard to analyze, let alone predict. Rational expectations can be made rationally with probabilities attached but, when assumptions fail, a new rationality or irrationality must be recognized.

Since human beings do not make decisions or choices in a vacuum, the real-life availability of goods and services is not constant, even daily. In theory, a perfect product or service available at an affordable cost at the ideal time and in the ideal location is perfect economics. Perfect economics is an enviable goal, but the best we can achieve is "better" and that goes for the spirit as well.

The power of the Holy Spirit in a man or woman certainly changes profit and moral preferences for the better. Fear, greed, activity, passivity, love, hate, compassion, indifference, and other emotional factors change, often markedly, when the Holy Spirit is involved. The Holy Spirit is that invisible force that knows the ultimate trade-offs, efficiencies, and objectives, nudging or forcing action as necessary. Sadly, the science of behavioral economists has not yet considered God as influential in each situation and, perhaps, never will.

Human Situational Awareness and God

Human situational awareness is itself hard to define, let alone measure. There are those of us who simply go along to get along, waiting for the wind to steer us in its chosen direction without any situational awareness. Some profit and some get blindsided. In contrast, many go out and try to grab all they can with no concern for proximate or remote consequences. Again, some profit and some get blindsided and some blindside others. Personalities, education, and experiences serve to improve decision-making, but awareness of God is the real difference maker.

Classic situational awareness training attempts to improve the prediction of outcomes by identifying influential elements that need addressed, by limiting distractions, by avoiding complacency, by seeing what others are doing and may do, by understanding the relevance of time in given situations, and by using feelings/intuition and analysis to predict events. It is not by coincidence that the military employs situational analysis to help combatants protect points of weaknesses; knowing weakness is the first step to building strength. The objective is to minimize uncontrollable concerns while creating them for the enemy.

Situational awareness includes self-interest which can be good or bad, sometimes, at the same time. No amount of altruism can change that. What we do not have should motivate us to create something better. Many see the self-interest conundrum as a matter of wants and needs, needs as being necessary and wants as being beyond that which we need. But if a man was to only produce as needed, there would be nothing for others who were not able to produce enough. The rational conclusion holds that every man and woman should produce as much as possible in economic and spiritual currency. Self-interest should not be random, neither should selfless interest. There is nothing random when it comes to God's interests.

Self-interest can produce idols. When man seeks to redefine the ideal definitions of money, character, passion or love, absent faithfulness to God, the love of those ideals can foster idols. Money, morals, character, and love do not have to be mutually exclusive. Character and money can be a powerful combination in pursuit of value for passion purposes, but temptation confronts those with the most money and passion every day. Neither the money one has, nor the character one exhibits is but a starting point for who one can be tomorrow or how much value can be created.

One idol that frequently appears in disguise is technology which is progressive in nature, yet often, creatively destructive. Technology can raise the spirit and improve efficiencies while, at the same time, it can divert attention from the important things in life. Technological advances come in waves, sometimes, in concert with man's attention to God. Ironically, God often uses the forces of creative destruction to correct attention deficits. Excess and obsolescence seem to be man's fate.

Risk aversion can become its own idol, holding back minds from pursuing significant opportunity. Humans have an innate aversion to change because of the fear of the unknown. Habits and automatic behavior patterns, repeated and learned by trial and experience, favor the status quo, existing systems, and easy pleasures. The incentive to change must be strong or "generally accepted practice" will remain for longer than its utility.

Control is man's quest to be like God. Men and women like to control change and to maintain control. They think that he who has most and knows best can control most, which is why power struggles over the material rage in every generation resulting in an atmosphere for either uneasy peace or war. Absent reverence to God, man aggressively reaches outward for more or becomes protective of his status quo.

Governments, in like fashion, do not prefer change unless it is down the path to more control. Governments author change using constituent self-interest (fear, greed, laziness, etc.) as motivators. New governments find quickly that people dislike loss more than they favor gain. Old governments attempt to keep the majority satisfied and devoid of major risk even when the costs of that satisfaction become more than are affordable. Herds of people who follow blindly those who would lead them astray end up in a box canyon and, overtime, stress comes to those in the herd who are at the bottom and then those in the middle of the food chain, followed by all.

Those who do not join blind herds recognize that each of us continue until death to be free to judge according to our own relative perceptions of values, risks, circumstances, and expectations. If choices are limited to two distinct cause and effect situations, most people will choose the more certain outcome. Choices among costs, benefits, and existing preferences will often default to a comfortable place. Because people think of value in relative rather than absolute terms, the "relative" squeezes out the "absolute" in both proximate and remote situations (both spiritual and material). It is worthy to note that God's absolutes also minimize the squeezing-out and dead-end progressions and enable each of us to maintain a more steady, orderly course.

Think about the nonlinear variables that come into play when choice matters. Then, think about how you and others you know make choices. Some know more, feel more, assume more, or are more motivated. Those variables are not easily measurable nor are potential synergies among them nor are the outcomes. Computers can game future possibilities, even probabilities, but inevitably, err in their predictions.

Those who study behavior know that intangibles can take over the decision-making process. To make the point, consider the following list of unrelated, yet sometimes, situationally related, one-line truths. Life's accomplishments come in season to the steadfast. Satisfaction is a desire that must be earned and cannot be transferred. Challenges are overcome when determination is not overcome by challenges. The middle of anything tempts us to turn back or not finish. Today's passion needs to be tomorrow's passion if anything is to come of it. The hard road is often easier than the easy road in making a complete journey. It is better to control an itch than to let it control you. In each case, attitude makes a difference. Accomplishment is an objective, satisfaction is a reward, situational challenges differ, and attitude and focus make the difference in both decisions and outcomes.

Trust is certainly one of the single most important factors in choosing one direction or person over another. It serves as a foundation for building relationships and markets. Trust comes and goes with experiences. Consistency in those experiences breeds the trust that leads to favorable commitment. It is easier to commit to something or someone you believe in. It is not so easy to trust when you have been deceived, when you experience performances that fail to meet expectations, when generally accepted norms have been violated, when hopes have been dashed, or when optimism turns to pessimism. Trust is a function of the quality of your relationships (and their sustainability) in spiritual and economic terms. Trust in God is a most significant decision factor.

Free Behavior Versus Controlled Behavior

On a macroeconomic level, the School of Austrian Economics is, in many ways, the opposite of the Keynesian/government control/influencer model for humanity. The Austrian School believes that markets are self-organizing and, therefore, should be left to organize without interference. Free markets beat government every time. Individuals acting in their own self-interest create exchanges with other self-interested parties. The exchange itself determines price and utility for those involved and those who would follow. The opportunity cost of either buying or foregoing a purchase factors into the choice, knowingly or unknowingly. Prices are functions of knowledge and can lead to scarcity. A rise in price tells the exchanger whether to exchange or not. Substitutes are sought and found when price becomes unbearable. New markets become established markets, and the prices therein are simply products of self-organizing human interaction.

Governments simply cannot create lasting exchanges that work. People in situations determine the best utility of the situation and make decision to exchange or not to exchange in the moment. Government may seek to foster better exchanges but rarely see either the reality of the situation or the ripple effect of the decisions made by participants. Opportunities, outside influences, subjective evaluations, and consequences are beyond the purview of government edicts issued from on high.

As with any economic decision, prices and availability depend on ownership and use rights. Commodities, including money, derive their value from the relative security that choices will be honored, utility will not be infringed, the asset can be quietly enjoyed while held, and a present or future transfer of the rights to the asset will be permitted. Economies are based on perceived guarantees including the right to own and to use a commodity throughout an ownership period. Once again, it is trust that enables markets to function freely in linear and nonlinear proportions. Trust is not engendered by human control agents who give and take away rights at will, thereby, influencing outcomes.

Markets and People are Organic in God's Economy

Markets for goods and services form within local and national economies either organically or by government design. Organic markets spring up locally first as products and services, capital, and intellect are put to work. Markets grow as increasing demand encourages more supply. Mature markets create expectations both for price and availability. The more mature a market and the more it grows beyond local boundaries, the more likely both private and governmental interests will seek to control it. Importantly, the same is true of noneconomic relationships as well.

For perspective, men and women are but players in a long-running organic drama. The central theme is that certain cast members commit to each other and to God while others do not. Of those who commit to God, many ultimately choose to turn away. Some of those who turn away turn back when they realize the folly of their turning. Throughout the story, God and His *Invisible Hand* are at work both in and behind the scenes whether the characters know how to define Him or not and, more importantly, whether they personally know Him or not.

The interesting plotline in any life or in any generation is centered on the trade-off between immediate, temporal rewards and long-term, even eternal rewards. Gratification itself is simple and complex at the same time. Investment in godly pursuits produce godly rewards in the moment and over generations but may likely not be evident in full to the choosers. Human investments in human causes rarely produce rewards that last a lifetime. Interestingly and ironically, God can and does use both the best and the worst of a man's or a woman's investments for his good pleasure and for purposes that last more than a lifetime. A life well-lived or a life poorly-lived can each create rewards for others.

Biblical rules for living are organic in application but not in intent. The Ten Commandments are straight to the point. The Beatitudes detail the rewards for "right" living. The two Great

19

Commandments never fail, regardless of circumstance. Yet, men invariably think they know a better way or, at least, a way to justify their material and spiritual choices. Those rules determine direction and, if that direction was unworthy, the rules would not stand as rules. Admittedly, an element of faith is required to stick with rules that seem inapplicable or uneasy, particularly when those around claim them to be unimportant.

"Thou shalt have no other gods before me" is the First Commandment. It is first because it is a requisite for all the rest. "Love the Lord with of all your heart, soul and mind" is Jesus' way of explaining how to serve God as the one and only God. Notice the order: heart, soul, and mind. The heart is the doorway to understanding. The mind rationalizes its way through the doorway. The ultimate recognition comes when the heart and soul see truth, embrace truth, and live truth, creating a higher level of multilevel situational awareness.

This is not to say that those who deeply love the Lord see clearly in all or even most things. Sin and error exist in all of us. Omniscience is nonexistent in man, however, becoming a partner in God's good purposes adds to vision and creates wisdom. Humble obedience to God makes personal economics simpler as noise is weeded out. Built into a partnership with God is a courage to do that which was previously hidden, unheeded, or feared in the proximate and for the remote.

Be AWARE (in every situation), **Be FAITHFUL** (to the living God) or **Be @RISK** from here forward presents thought-provoking insights and arguments concerning a wide array of subjects faced situationally by each of us every day. The topics are spiritual, yet economic; directional, yet reflective; and human but God-centric. Pointed questions are asked to heighten your situational awareness, your thoughtful analysis, and your concerted action. The topics and the situations cited are by no means complete in themselves nor are they all-encompassing beyond themselves. Collectively, they offer a beginning for reflection on your life or on the lives of those around you. Time, space, and material elements may differ in your specific circumstance but your awareness of each topic and the world around you can lead you to pray specifically for insight and wisdom as the Lord would provide.

The topical headings serve as a reference guide for those experiencing a crisis of understanding. The quick-hitting proverbs, relevant admonitions, intrusive questions, subtle ironies, situational warnings, preferred mindsets, disciplines, common sense, sound investitures, judgments, basic economics of life, decision trade-offs, money matters, and, most importantly, God-speak are intended to develop your thoughtfulness. You may feel that you are being exposed to a box of chocolates, not knowing which taste comes next. But each taste in the assortment offers an opportunity to seek and learn. God reveals to those who seek. Those who learn will apply and multiply His purposes.

The more you apply your mind to this "awareness exercise," the more you will begin to know yourself, your situation, and your opportunities to make the proximate and the remote better understood and better for many. Use the thoughts presented and add your own considered interpretations. Truths will become clearer with prayer and practice. Personal and economic relationships will become more substantive. Others will be attracted to your wisdom and witness. The life you live will be blessed, and you will bless others. Importantly, God will notice your sincerity and commitment and lend an *Invisible Hand* in His way and in His time.

Awareness topics are organized into three categories that transition from the spiritual condition of a soul to the practical economics facing that soul, leading to the geopolitical and macroeconomic situations in which we find ourselves. *Spiritual Awareness, Life Economics Awareness, and Macro Economic and Geopolitical Awareness* are separate, yet complementary. The three are intertwined in human life. Matters of the spirit really do influence economics and vice versa. Individual spiritual inclinations and business economics can and do influence macroeconomic policies and directions and vice versa.

Spiritual Awareness should provide a mindset, one that should be alive and constructive in good times and trying times. *Life Economics Awareness* helps a mind and body to survive and to thrive, supported by a right spirit. *Macroeconomic and Geopolitical Awareness* is a summary view of both proximate and remote trends and events, considering the temptations, distractions, and speculations that can overcome every man and woman and every society.

Throughout history, both the advantaged and the disadvantaged have forfeited opportunity and freedom when macro and micro senses became clouded. Dark clouds inherently appear when God has been diminished. History shows us how the process works. Being aware of what exists and distinguishing it from what should exist under God is the first step to knowing what comes next and what may then come next after that. Situational awareness always recognizes that time limits us but not the purposes of God. Though the season in which we live is interesting, if not chaotic, God's rules for order work. In this season in time, God's rules for order have been de-emphasized in favor of man's futile attempts to create a new secular order. A cancer has grown within the hearts and minds of those who prefer that human order over God's. The cancer that has taken root in this season in social, political, and economic institutions has created disorder in hearts and nations across the globe. Creative destruction is thereby increasing at an increasing rate, spinning seemingly out of control as the controllers of human order become trapped by inescapable dilemmas created by their own hands. Our current times may not be the "end of times," but we are certainly headed for trying times. Be aware, be vigilant, and be content with whatever comes. The most trying of times provide the greatest opportunities for growth, for service, and for witness.

Reader Alert

Please do not read the short, sometimes pithy, insights for selected spiritual, personal, economic, and macro-political economic topics presented herein for reflection and inspiration as you would a novel. Each one begs you to think and, specifically, to think about yourself in context. You may have already pondered some of the insights herein and faithfully apply them in your life. Other topics and insights may be totally new to you. Take your time and surprise yourself by your own insightful observations as God reveals them to you. One or two topics a day will increase your awareness of that which is not obvious. Trust the process and absorb what you learn from looking at and listening to the world around you. As knowledge and self-knowledge grow, wisdom will come upon you. Importantly, ask God to show you what is important for His purposes in the rest of your life.

As you read, you will note that certain Biblical words/ phrases/ concepts have been incorporated into the text. Whenever a full verse appears in quotation marks, its Book, Chapter and/or Verse is cited immediately following for your further reference.

I. Spiritual Awareness in Theory and Practice

Awareness grows as the mind and spirit work in concert to see a situation, its participants, and potential outcomes. As you face your situations, consider the *think points* and the *soul points* presented in the one-line statements, proverbs, questions, warnings, and admonitions for your use. Theory profits no one unless put into practice. The *think points* and the *soul points* are not segregated within the topics that follow to allow you to decide for yourself which thought and which inner sense or combination of the two to use to your advantage or the advantages of others. Unawareness is not a viable option.

1. Wisdom is Often Elusive within the Best of Situations.

"If any of you lacks wisdom, he should ask God, who generously gives to all without finding fault, and it will be given to him."

—James 1:5

- Wisdom finds the lost and the found, rarely equally.
- Every situation begs for wisdom, but often, it is not timely in its appearance.
- Expect wisdom to appear in the least likely places from the least likely sources.
- Wisdom is often simple, sometimes complex, and always needed.
- Wisdom can be distorted beyond recognition by those who would rule.
- Wisdom grows when we muffle the irrelevant and hear the discordant while quieting the noise in us and around us.
- What we think we know today is rarely what is or what we will embrace tomorrow.
- Wisdom matters not only to those who seek it but to those who stray from it.
- Happiness should never be valued above wisdom.
- Take no solace in the "lesser of two evils" for evil creates no solace.
- Each blessing and trial have been given to us for a reason, often beyond our understanding.
- False narratives diminish the quest for truth in those without discernment.
- Good advice should result in the passing on of good advice.
- Superior intellect is not an end-in-itself, the application of wisdom is.
- Men are not born with wisdom nor is there a guarantee of finding an adequate amount.
- Wisdom sometimes just appears when nature exposes it, difficulty forces it, or others model it.

- God created wisdom to be used today for tomorrow's benefit.
- If wisdom and understanding begin and end with God, He can be found at its core.
- Black can appear as white, and white can be turned black in minds full of gray.
- Relying on human understanding alone is never enough.

2. What Do You Think About?

"Then you will know the truth, and the truth will set you free."

—John 8:32

- Do you think about what you want to buy more than what you can create to sell?
- Do you think about how much you take the water you drink for granted?
- Do you think more about your successes or your failures?
- Do you think about all those empires that have come and gone, and why?
- Do you think about your neighbors' needs and wants or your own?
- Do you think about ease, difficulty, and points in between?
- Do you think about both scarcity and abundance with gratitude?
- Do you think about nature and man's nature as both change before your eyes?
- Do you think about consequences before you act or react or afterward?
- Do you think about God in more than a passing moment?

3. The Obvious and The Not-So Obvious Are with Us Nevertheless.

"For my thoughts are not your thoughts, neither are my ways your ways, declares the Lord."

—Isaiah 55:8

"To whom much is given, much is required" does not translate as "To whom little is given, little is required." Those who think little, end up with just a little. Those who do little, end up doing for others but a little. Big and little things are often sized by how big or little we are. Then again, the big things come from God, and the little things come from us. With God, doing becomes a way of life which causes things to happen, profiting both the obvious and the not-so obvious. Midst it all, God instructs us to know ourselves and our times, lest we remain complacent. Complacency is the enemy of every season in life, however obvious or unobvious.

4.   Man's Linear versus God's Nonlinear Thinking

"He is a double-minded man, unstable in all he does."

—James 1:8

- Man struggles with the nonlinear and is confused by God's use of the linear for nonlinear purposes.
- Man optimizes in the now while God optimizes over generations.
- Hoarding and speculation (fear and greed) are born of man's confusion about the basics.
- Cycles exist to convince man that he must live beyond the situationally comfortable.
- Shifting sands cannot be fortified with linear foundations.
- Multiple circumstances and people are used by God for more than linear purposes.
- Servants who supply, reap more than they supply in the moment.
- "Cause and effect" look linear until God shows up.
- Nature overrules man's views, expectations, control, and power when least expected.
- Myopic minds focus on the material and, often, miss the fullness of eternity.

5. **Biblical Principles from Proverbs and the Prophet in Ecclesiastes for Eternity and Today.**

> *"Whatever exists has already been named and what man is has been known...."*
> —Ecclesiastes 6:10

- "Better is the end of a thing than its beginning."
- "Anger lodges in the hearts of fools."
- "God has made adversity and prosperity."
- "Not one righteous man who does good never sins."
- "Vanity in any form or circumstance is evil."
- "The race does not go to the swift...the battle to the strong...bread to the wise...riches to the intelligent...favor to those with knowledge...but time and chance happen to them all."
- "Death and life lie in the power of the tongue."
- "One rebuke to one of understanding is better than 100 blows to a fool."
- "A joyful heart is good medicine while a crushed spirit dries up bones."

Perspective lies in wait for each of us. We often get sidetracked by preoccupations, yet those preoccupations often tell the tale of a soul's storyline on earth. The only storyline that matters is our struggle to keep our short time one earth in perspective, using what we have been given while waiting for God to reveal just a little more about eternity.

6.   **Success and Failure Are More About the Definition of Each and the Sustainability of the Other.**

"The wise in heart are called discerning..."
—Proverbs 16:21

Opposites attract, perhaps no more than when it comes to success and failure. Since we define success as good and failure as bad, most people would choose success. Unfortunately, success comes with failure and failure can be a by-product of success. Our successes and failures show us the way to succeed if we do not get caught-up with the successes or failures themselves. The definition of each really depends on the purpose undertaken, the effort given, and the degree to which we allow God to have a role in our successes and failures.

7. **Growing Up Has Always Been Hard to Do, Yet We Must to Prosper.**

> *"And the child grew and became strong; he was filled with wisdom, and the grace of God was upon him."*
>
> —Luke 2:40

- Parents can be good and bad models; hold on to the good and let go of the bad.
- Strive to do what is right despite pressures, misconceptions, and the advice of others.
- Your next attempt at being a teenager or an adult-teenager may spoil your next attempt at being an adult.
- Beware of those people and things that destroy lives.
- Before you fight, fight through the impulse just to fight for the sake of anger.
- Always remember that God created you for a present and future purpose.
- Real adults do not commit adultery.
- Knowing "right" is more important than testifying about who is right.
- Listening translates into understanding if both sides listen enough to understand.

8. Questions for Those Seeking Ultimate Value in Creation.

> *"Life is more than food, and the body more than clothes."*
>
> —Luke 12:23

- If you owned the earth and those that dwell therein, what value would you add to or subtract from your domain?
- What descriptors would you use to define the value of your purpose in life?
- Where does good and evil begin and end in the situation at hand?
- How would righteousness, justice, and equity change under your control?
- How much freedom would you permit; how much free stuff would you provide?
- Would you reward or punish in the moment, over time, or not at all?
- Would your world consist of a single matrix or a collection of unique parts, systems, and souls?
- What priority would you give to acquired human wisdom?
- Would you favor one person over another and for what duly important reason?
- What value can you and should you add during your remaining time on earth?

9.   What Are Your Rights Worth?

"Live as free men, but do not use your freedom
as a cover-up for evil; live as servants of God."
—1 Peter 2:16

A *right* is a privilege, a benefit, an immunity from something or someone, or an advantage for a time or for all time. Rights may be granted, earned, inherited, or taken. Rights can make us free from certain obligations or liabilities. Rights, in most cases, are valuable assets. Many rights can be conveyed to others with compensation or not.

Rights associated with a physical asset are often valued by the economic returns generated by that asset in the present and over time. Spiritual rights are less tangible, sometimes described as goodwill and valued beyond that which human use can measure.

Think about the rights you possess. Those rights may have physical or human limits which limit the worthiness of those rights. For example, if you own real estate in the United States, you have the legal right to use it, to enjoy it without interference, and to sell or transfer it. If you own a stash of money, you have the right to save it, to spend it, or to invest it. You are limited by the size of the stash of cash you have and its ultimate purchasing power.

Your right to life is worth something too. It may be limited by time, by your physical or mental condition, and by your attitude/ gratitude, but you control its applied value. Assess whether your life could be worth more or less? You have the right to make it more valuable to yourself and to others but, often, may not.

10. Rights and Responsibilities Are Personal and Economic Opposites.

> *"Let us not become weary in doing good, for at the proper time we will reap a harvest if we do not give up."*
>
> —Galatians 6:9

Inalienable rights (inherent and inviolable) breed inalienable responsibilities (situational and eternal). There is nothing inalienable about rights or responsibilities except that which is in the mind. We employ our rights or fulfill our responsibilities as we choose. What we deserve as a result is another matter.

Everyone has lists of demands from cradle to grave. We want love, health, harmony on our terms, and the freedom to do as we find necessary or pleasurable. We sometimes offer gratitude for what we have. We sometimes act responsibly. But we rarely consider what we deserve.

Thinking about rights and responsibilities should lead us to ask:

1. Who gave you the right to life when you were born into this world?
2. What reasonable demands and responsibilities should apply to yourself and others?
3. Who owns the right and responsibility for your thoughts, words, and deeds?
4. Who will convey what rights to you on your deathbed?
5. Who ultimately values the use of your inalienable rights used during your time on earth?
6. What do you sow, and what shall you reap?

11. Vanity Cannot Exist in God's Economy.

"This is what the Lord says: What fault did your fathers find in me that they strayed so far from me? They followed worthless idols and became worthless themselves."

—Jeremiah 2:5

Vanity stalks each of us. It is not just for the beautiful people. It is a disease within each of us, often exhibited when thinking we are immune. Ecclesiastes says, "All is vanity," which refers to our mindset as well as all that we do. The bottom-line economics of vanity are simple: a fruitless endeavor produces no fruit. Vanity may feel good to the mind in the moment; however, those feel good moments are just moments and may ultimately be counterproductive.

The supply of vanity seems endless in our politicians, our educators, our celebrities, and our neighbors, but as we exclude and excuse ourselves by comparison, the resulting judgment is itself vain. Perhaps that is why God reserves judgment for Himself.

The Seven Deadly Sins (greed, gluttony, lust, pride, sloth, envy, and wrath) are by-products of vanity. We chase many a sinful wind that blows. When the wind stops, the calm enables us to see the ravages left behind in the pursuit to others and to ourselves. However, "seeing" comes only to those who choose to see vanity for what it is.

Vanity loves to be in control. In control, we can view ourselves with our own lens. Self-righteousness blurs the line between vanity and righteousness, missing the imperfections in ourselves as we point to the shortcomings of others. God knocks us off our stalking horse in His way, in His time.

12. Irony Is Not Always Humorous.

"Why, you do not even know what will happen tomorrow. What is your life? You are a mist that appears for a little while and then vanishes."

—James 4:14

- Irony is not ironic when it could or should have been expected.
- Irony teaches us to expect the unexpected in all human endeavors, including science.
- Irony may be most ironic when obvious, yet not understood.
- Little ironies can turn into little problems or big learning opportunities.
- Irony for one may not translate into irony for many; however, irony for nations often translates into consequences for everyone.
- The irony of effort is that even good effort can produce better and poorer than anticipated results on one or multiple levels.
- Individuals act efficiently when free to act in perceived non-efficient ways.
- Free will is God's unique gift at birth, a flight of fancy in youth, a tool for good or evil in adulthood, and an ironic determinant of salvation in eternity.

13. Ironically, the Noise You Hear May Be Your Own.

"O town full of commotion"....beware of your own noise.

—Isaiah 22:2

Trying to serve two masters at the same time gets noisy. The harder we work for one master, the less we have left to give to the other. People of all stripes typically want to be the master of souls but find, not always quickly, that God has claim to that which man cannot understand or measure. We often allow our wants or our needs to become our master, relegating God to merely being a background noise in our minds. Our ever-moving targets, changing environments, spent energies, time and money wasted are noises. Complaints and worries about noise produce little but more complaint, worry, or listless sleep. Life is often harder until we learn that we are the noise. When we quiet that noise in ourselves, we begin to see God modulating the physical, economic, and spiritual noise throughout creation.

14. God Has Told Us His Story for a Reason.

"For the message of the cross is foolishness to those who are perishing, but to us who are being saved it is the power of God."

—1 Corinthians 1:18

His Story is the foundation of all of history despite man's attempts to minimize it, dispute it, and recreate it. God's Word has been written to pierce ready and non-ready hearts with truths deeper than physical nature. As the Word deepens our understanding, it prompts us a to higher calling, to become less foolish and to lead others by testimony and, by example, to faith. God is the author of each story for it serves His grand purpose.

15. When God Looks at a Human Life, He Knows the Unvarnished Truth.

> *"Whoever believes in him is not condemned,*
> *but whoever does not believe stands condemned*
> *already...."*
>
> —John 3:18

- Men cannot hide in secret places.
- Those devoted to myths do nothing for the world or the devotee.
- The gift of free choice is diminished when not applied under God.
- God knows the plans He has for you and they are better than yours.
- Man's attempt at stardom is limited by clinging to his humanity.
- Love is ever-needed, ever-changing, and ever-pursued but not truly found until given.
- God calls each of us to be stewards of men and women as well as money.
- God supplies larger doses of wisdom for those who would create a better reality.
- Weaknesses and strengths are bestowed to create more strength than weakness.
- Unbelief in God spells unrest in life and sadness for God.

16. Seeing a Situation Clearly Involves the Mind and the Heart at the Same Time.

> *"For since the creation of the world God's invisible qualities-his eternal power and divine nature-have been clearly seen, being understood from what has been made, so that men are without excuse."*
>
> —Romans 1:20

- Seeing the contrary can be good if the contrariness is not for personal aggrandizement.
- Absent clarity from God, thinking clearly is not possible.
- We never know where we will find God, especially when not looking.
- Total blindness is the absence of sight and insight.
- Blindness to God is not about eyesight or mindsight but heart sight.
- Seeing after being blind reveals a sea of blind spots.
- Seeing is as much about the seer as the sight.
- The more jaded our thoughts, the less we comprehend or feel.
- Clarity reveals that there are no guarantees or entitlements in life.
- Knowing that God "is" is not as knowing as who God "is."

17. Grace Is Often Unseen, Unappreciated, and Unwelcomed by Ungraceful Men.

"From the fullness of his grace we have all received one blessing after another."
—John 1:16

God's grace is never absent nor is it powerless. With grace, forgiveness is not blind to judgment; it merely blinds the judgment of the one who forgives. Mercy then is a gift, not an obligation, given freely in lieu of judgment. Mercy is not a typical human trait. It may be acquired. It may be seen in others and then passed on. It often lies latent until the right moment. Yet, we are called to make every moment a-mercy-and-a-forgiveness moment.

Forgiveness and being forgiven are opposites that produce complementary results. Repentance is the other side of forgiveness and requires not just words but action. Ungraceful men and women prefer to be forgiven but are not generally forgiving. Free from retribution, freedom given can be used for a new good or a continuance of the old bad. That is where graceful learning begins.

Forgiving by no means justifies sin. Permitting the sinner to recommit the sin without consequence indulges the behavior, if only in the sinner's mind. Forgiveness can benefit both the forgiver and the forgiven if the forgiven comprehends what has been forgiven and appreciates the mercy given.

18. **Situational Happiness Depends on Talents and Resources Put to Good Use.**

> *"We all have different gifts, according to the grace given us. If a man's gift is prophesying, let him use it in proportion to his faith. If it is serving, let him serve; if it is teaching, let him teach; if it is encouraging, let him encourage; if it is contributing to the needs of others, let him give generously; if it is leadership, let him govern diligently; if it is showing mercy, let him do it cheerfully."*
>
> —Romans 12:6

Happiness is a state of mind, not an ultimate objective. We all want it, try to make it, or take it and end up wondering why it did not last. Happiness in life comes to us and stays with us when we make other lives better. It is then that happiness expands into joy. The ultimate joy is *joy in the Lord* which visits us moment by moment as we enjoy the fruits of our labors and His purposes. In contrast, vanity often lies hidden in the pursuit of happiness and serves as a barrier to joy. Talents and resources put to good use for others may be vanity driven but not when a godly purpose drives the effort and exertion.

19. The Economics of Prayer Are More Powerful Than We Are Aware.

> *"If my people who are called by my name, will humble themselves and pray and seek my face and turn from their wicked ways, then will I hear from heaven and will forgive their sin and will heal their land."*
>
> —2 Chronicles 7:14

When in need, a heart gravitates to prayer, especially when obvious answers escape us. Many hearts though do not naturally gravitate to prayer because of doubts about the power on the other end. The closer a heart lives to God, the closer we come to live by praying daily. Praising and thanking God is a good introduction. Humility shows that we recognize who is in control. "Let me understand my needs and your desires and the differences between the two" leads a heart to ask for the appropriate amount of the needs. Waiting for an answer is the hard part.

Prayers for provision, forgiveness, repentance, and deliverance should be ongoing occurrences. Daily prayer shows a seriousness of faith among believers. A prayer for discernment should be a continuing request. The more aware a prayer, the more explicit the request and, while God hears all requests, He often blesses those who pray with a better understanding of what is being asked. Diligent prayers improve the economics of praying.

Note that the economics of prayer reveal that the prayers of two or more multiply the responses from God. When two or more are gathered, synergies result. Being thankful for blessings goes a long way toward being blessed. Praying and including others on a regular basis fosters relationships that bless. Everyone in the prayer circle should ultimately pray a prayer like this: "Lord, please give me just what I require to keep You foremost." And He will!

20. The Results of Prayer Are Hard to Quantify until You See Them Firsthand.

> *"If you remain in me and my words remain in you, ask whatever you wish, and it will be given to you."*
>
> —John 15:7

- Recognize up front that no man or woman deserves a God who listens.
- Prayer does not always result in prayed for outcomes but, often unexpectedly, preferred results.
- Quantifying the results of prayer is difficult because prayers seek an expected response, and God often provides a better alternative.
- Answers to prayer always point to the need to keep praying.
- Answers to prayer sometimes create more questions than answers which may be the point.
- Prayer reveals as much about the awareness of the prayer as the prayer itself.
- Prayer is not a justification for lazy action but inspires perseverance.
- Bottom line: never let an opportunity to pray go to waste!

21.   The Bible Emphasizes the Word "Not" for Every Situation.

> *"Thou shalt not have idols, take the name of the Lord in vain, murder, commit adultery, steal, bear false witness, covet."*

—Exodus 20:2-17

Breaking God's commandments may not result in immediate consequences; however, both consequences and unintended consequences are set in motion. The Old Testament gave us rules that work in lives and nations. Disobedience spells disaster. The New Testament gave us Jesus and forgiveness with new rules that build on the old. Jesus emphasized the *dos* in life as well as the *do nots* for navigating both calm and stormy seas. Sins of omission and sins of commission are equally offensive in God's sight. Jesus modeled "meek and mild" but also "strong and commanding," using the words "do" and "not" many times in emphasizing the consequences of *doing* what you should *not* or *not doing* what you should.

22. Order and Disorder Evidence a Constant Battle Between Opposites.

"For God is not a God of disorder but of peace."
—1 Corinthians 14:33

Order and disorder play out in man's economy every day. Order never lasts while disorder rarely ends. Reality is always on the move, keeping mankind guessing. Forming and deforming are opposites that attract and destroy each other, sometimes at the same time. Entropy can work both ways; order and disorder correct each other, creating a new order while, sometimes, leaving remnants of the old. The energy that it takes to preserve an existing order is often misspent.

Randomness is not disorder; often, it is part of God's hidden order. God quietly or not-so-quietly turns wrong into right, unseen into evident, and ironic into true. He allows disorder to reform order when the existing order is ordered apart from His will or His timing. Remember that order evolves in every situation from contrary viewpoints and disorder erupts from being contrary. Train your mind to see both.

23. Reputations Are Valuable for Every Situation.

"A good name is more desirable than great riches;
to be esteemed is better than silver or gold."
—Proverbs 22:1

- Reputations change personal and economic relationships.
- Make yourself favorably memorable to everyone you meet.
- Your worth to yourself and to others is worth fighting for.
- You are uniquely qualified to tell the truth and untruth about yourself.
- Your resume tells what you have been while your persona tells who you are.
- Reputation is about more than economics, yet economic actions verify reputations.
- Promises made and commitments kept build a reputation like nothing else can.

24. Questioning Your God-Awareness Quotient

"Now we see but a poor reflection; then we shall see face to face. Now I know in part; then I shall know fully, even as I am fully known."
—1 Corinthians 13:12

- Does God's abiding love enable everyone to go to Heaven?
- Do good works on earth justify a place in Heaven?
- Was God's choice of those who will choose salvation in Jesus Christ known from the beginning?
- Does God hate sins of all varieties and degrees?
- Is God's omnipotence, omnipresence, and omniscience undeniable?
- Do God's commandments work for the obedient and against the disobedient?
- Do you take time to embrace or deny the power of the Holy Spirit?
- Was the Bible inspired by God through the hearts and hands of its multigenerational authors?
- Is the final judgment of your soul a scary proposition?
- Is Satan a real power hell-bent on confusing, tempting, and misdirecting mankind?
- Does the guilt of others stick with you more than your own?
- Does your view of God color your view of men and women?

25. The Situational Economics of Wants and Needs.

"And my God will meet all your needs according to his glorious riches in Christ Jesus."
—Philippians 4:19

- If what you want for you is not what you want for others, both you and the want warrant introspection.
- Self-interest is a right that does not have to trump the wants or needs of others.
- Gaining advantage for our wants and needs is not created by not doing.
- Those who simplify much for the wants and needs of many profit this world.
- Reasonability is that place where wants and needs meet at the practical.
- Shortages in life essentials lessen the demand for nonessentials.
- The more tangible our wants, the more likely the motivation to obtain them.
- Wants become needs the further we distance ourselves from reality.
- Self-interest is not random which means that selfless interest is not random either.
- Self-interest is not always about winning the best economic, emotional, or spiritual deal.

26. **Parenting Is a Situation That Demands More than a Little Supply.**

> *"Train a child in the way he should go, and when he is old he will not turn from it."*
>
> —Proverbs 22:6

- Fathers and mothers are important in complementary ways; therefore, do not voluntarily seek to be your opposite. *Kids need both.*
- If you want to be head of the household, do not marry one. *Kids are confused by two at odds.*
- Maturity is more important in parents than kids. *Kids need to learn maturity by seeing it in action.*
- Someone must be the glue in every family for the family to remain a family. *Kids need glue that sticks.*
- Honoring of father and mother builds character when each strives to be worthy of honor. *Be worthy in building your kid's character.*
- Biblical parenting is time tested; new techniques come into vogue and are gone. *Kids need an interesting Bible story every day to keep Satan at bay.*

27. Going After Things That Do *Not* Profit.

"What good is it for a man to gain the whole world, yet forfeit his soul?"

—Mark 8:36

- Man pursues man-made gods, even though they are gods that change during the pursuit.
- Rationalization leads to profits unrealized or foregone.
- Lawlessness results in profits unobtained and losses unanticipated.
- The pleasures of unrighteousness create an increasing emptiness in men and women.
- Stay away from those who walk in idleness.
- Being busy at work is good; being a busybody is counterproductive.
- A fear of the Lord leads to wisdom which leads to endeavors that profit.
- Those with material wealth often neglect the higher rewards in life.
- The faithless repeat or multiply their losses.
- Eternal profit lies in the righteousness gained from every good work and word.
- Value the oxygen you breathe and the love given and received as undeserved profit.
- Those who sow more and better, reap more and better and earn joy in the results.

28. God Is More than Aware of Lawless Hearts.

"Everyone who sins breaks the law; in fact, sin is lawlessness."

—1 John 3:4

- All human objects of worship are deceiving.
- Lawless hearts lose situational discernment the further apart from God they travel.
- Sin keeps good and God away.
- Lawless prophets prophesy falsely, creating listeners who are hard of hearing.
- The lawless think laws to be arbitrary and at their discretion.
- Pure hearts and sincere faith resonate more with God than public acclamations and alms.
- The lawless applaud their humanity when convenient and self-serving.
- Hearts must remove lawless things prior to "returning to God."
- God allows lawless hearts to be hardened by standing aside for a time.
- Legalism often conflicts with a heartfelt awareness of God's commandments.

29. Accounting Is for Assets, Liabilities, and Souls.

"But I tell you that men will have to give account on the day of judgment for every careless word they have spoken."

—Matthew 12:36

Generally accepted accounting practice rules measure the health of an enterprise. Standardized measures of profits, losses, assets, and liabilities provide to the public, banks, governments, and owners a detailed summary of what has been and what exists today. There is no guarantee that future results will be an extension of the past, but trends are observable.

Accounting for the past and present health of a soul is different. The *divine accountant* knows the numbers perfectly, according to his *generally accepted rules for life practice*. He does not want to hold our liabilities against us and will forgive them if we ask. Meanwhile, the assets we have been given are for his use, not our own. Divine accounting is the end game.

30. Taking Can Be Theft in Many Kinds of Situations.

"The thief comes only to steal and kill and destroy...."

—John 10:10

- Theft is not limited to material things.
- Time is stolen by those who care little for the value of another person's time.
- Theft of innocence is a most grievous act.
- Character assassination is theft by intent.
- A person's spirit can be stolen, especially by those with little care for wisdom.
- Theft is taking something not rightfully due the taker for any reason in any situation.
- The laws of men cannot legislate against theft in many spiritual forms.
- Expect theft, protect against it where you can, and worry not where you cannot.

31. Nature or Nurture or an Awareness of God in Both?

"We urge you, brothers, warn those who are idle, encourage the timid, help the weak, be patient with everyone."

—1 Thessalonians 5:14

- Nurture is sometimes controlled by man, nature not so much.
- Real beauty lies in both nature and nurture, but beholders often fail to see it or mislabel it.
- Some brains are smart, some are not; both can nurture effectively when the spirit is willing.
- Neither nature nor nurture guarantee material wealth.
- Discipline is learned by nurture and, sometimes, forced by nature.
- The quest for *grace* is a function of nature and nurture working in lockstep.
- Holiness is nature and nurture coming together for a divine marriage.
- Forgiveness does not come naturally in nature or nurture.

32. Marriage Requires Awareness More than Feeling.

"Many a man claims to have unfailing love,
but a faithful man who can find?"

—Proverbs 20:6

- Common goals work best for marriage economics.
- Initial attractions can grow old quickly if allowed to languish in mediocrity.
- Forgiveness is a daily essential in marriage economics.
- Your significant other will reflect either the best or the worst of you.
- Financial realities often require disciplined decisions whether reality is real to all or not.
- Fidelity, loyalty, and sacrifice are critical investitures in any partner.
- Buyer's remorse is not the makings of a lasting marriage.
- Be slow to anger and great in wisdom for the best marriage learning experiences.
- Never let a day go by without gratitude for and thanks to your spouse and God.
- Synergy, both inside and outside a marriage, grows when supply is greater than expected.

33. Right and Wrong Are Not in the Eye of the Beholder.

"All a man's ways seem right to him, but the Lord weighs the heart."

—Proverbs 21:2

- The Ten Commandments are intentionally misinterpreted to justify errant human behavior.
- Consistent righteousness is impossible for the human heart.
- Repentance can help right a wrong only if the repentance translates into action.
- The Holy Spirit enables blind eyes to distinguish right from wrong.
- Doing "right" does not eliminate obstacles and suffering, but it does expand opportunities.
- Deceptions fool smart men in even the simplest of situations.
- Wisdom is far more profitable than being right.
- Earthly wisdom, counsel, and understanding cannot see through God's lens.
- Never be hasty with your righteousness when diligence is needed.
- "Right" can simply be investing the least for the greatest benefit.
- Risk grows exponentially for fools who are always right.
- Integrity is right; injustice is wrong; both can be seen differently by the best of us.
- The best course is to be righteous and not tell others how righteous you are.
- Consecration is a continuing process which grows the more we embrace it.
- The more we practice a sin, the more we rationalize its acceptable presence.

34. Truth and Judgment Require Awareness of Each Other.

"Then you will know the truth and the truth
will set you free."

—John 8:32

Truth and judgment produce different results stemming from different objectives. Freedom enables man to discover truth, complementary truth, or the opposite truth from which to judge. Judgments produce choices which require a will and a cost to act. Examine all sides in every decision to discover the truths and judgments inherent in each.

Be aware that truth lies in every corner of creation, waiting to be seen, embraced, and witnessed to others. True may not be true enough if enough is not known about the whole truth. Truth and untruth are opposites while fair and unfair are case specific. Human thoughts conflate or distort truth and fairness. We should expect truth to be known and liars with it despite attempts to conceal that which is untrue.

God is the author of truth and greatly to be heard, yet often unacceptably dissonant to our ears. God is the only author who transcends the beginning and end of each story. When His truth is hidden, conflated, or neglected, justice and righteousness stand at a distance. For man, when truth turns to lies, more lies follow as a man digs a spiritual or economic hole that must be scaled to escape. In contrast, when truth is evident, wisdom, discipline, and understanding grow. Those that buy into a Godly truth do not sell it but share it.

The economics of justice are these: we deserve it; we often demand it for others; and God rightly supplies both truth and justice for us in perfect time. Our free will is a catalyst for creating both good and evil in and apart from ourselves often concurrently. The good news is that anyone who pursues truth can be restored.

35. God Is Not Random Nor Is His Creation.

"For every house is built by someone, but God is the builder of everything."

—Hebrews 3:4

- Randomness is a most oversold explanation for those seeking to explain the unexplainable.
- The argument of randomness quells fear until "random" becomes a pattern.
- In physics and matters of the spirit, little is random.
- Complexity needs "random" excuses when understanding is limited.
- Not every random action produces a systemic response, but adjustment is required.
- Economics do not change randomly but may change the state of confusion.
- Integrity is not random; faith should not be random either.
- Wealth in this life or the next can be both randomly and intentionally earned.
- The Bible helps many believers deal with the unexpected, random or not.

36. Grading in Heaven Is Fortunately Above Our Pay Grade.

"You, therefore, have no excuse, you who pass judgment on someone else, for at whatever point you judge the other, you are condemning yourself, because you who pass judgment do the same things."
—Romans 2:1

The best judge knows the law and case-specific details intimately. No man possesses more than a glimpse of understanding. Men grade other men based on the material and the spirit in the moment. God knows all, the material and the immaterial, the moment and previous and future moments, and His good purpose.

Heaven is a place for those who qualify. Heaven is for the spirit made holy who have been saved from their unholiness. Heaven cannot be holy if the unholy are permitted to enter as is. Heaven is the ultimate destination, and the gates to Heaven open on demand but not by the demands of those who are approaching them. Entry is granted on a pass or fail basis. If men were to grade, knowing the truths and judgments of those seeking entry, the gates of Heaven would ungracefully remain shut a very, very long time.

37. The Myths of Situational Independence.

"Now the Lord is the Spirit, and where the Spirit of the Lord is, there is freedom."
—2 Corinthians 3:17

- The human mind fantasizes that sin does not matter or can be overcome by man alone.
- Men generally refuse the need for God and for wisdom until injured by life.
- History suggests time and again that with man alone at the helm all boats sink.
- The laws of *supply and demand* depend on the rationality of many more than one.
- Nothing is free, particularly independence.
- Fear and greed, the evil twins, are not independent.
- Rationalizations and misestimations often distort the meaning of independence.
- Fools think independence, aka self-reliance, to be their ticket to a happy life.
- Independence is not found in political, social, or economic correctness.
- Independence is not a matter of economics.
- Dependence on the world reduces the independence offered by God.

38. The Situation Is: You Did Not Choose God, He Chose You.

*"You did not choose me, but I chose you to go
and bear fruit - fruit that will last."*

—John 15:16

- God chose faithful followers before the beginning of time and watches them over time.
- Man likes to think that he has the power to choose, not just the freedom to choose.
- For context, "Where were you when God created the heavens and the earth?"
- Human definitions of God pale in comparison to his essence.
- The seasons of life change human thoughts but not God's chosen purpose for you.
- Why would an all-powerful God sacrifice so much to save a wretch like me?
- If you feel God at work within you, He has chosen to be there.
- If you think you can earn your way to being chosen, you are sorely mistaken.

39. A Biblical Prescription for Situational Awareness.

"For I know my transgressions, and my sin is always before me."

—Psalms 51:3

- Eternal salvation is first and foremost no matter the situation.
- Forgiveness is unburdening.
- The Word offers hope and awareness for living.
- Prayer is a means to the end of a righteous objective.
- Peace passes all understanding, but the peace must be just.
- Provision is guaranteed, better than what should be expected.
- Giving results in receiving abundantly.
- Future generations must learn faith, hope, and love.
- Follow this prescription and others will see it and want it.

40. Righteousness Is a Constant Battle.

"As it is written, there is no one righteous, not even one."

—Romans 3:10

Righteousness does not come naturally; yet, righteousness always rewards. There are no human experts on the subject; yet all humans respond to kindness whether given first or received in return. Unrighteousness (a.k.a. sin) is the great equalizer of unequal men. Evil has a way of seeking the path of least resistance to perpetuate itself in all men. Situations arise that call for righteousness; yet, few answer the call because we are deceived by our own definitions of righteousness. Interestingly, God uses man's unrighteous acts, deserving of damnation, for purposes of righteousness and salvation. The simple way out of the battle is to worship Christ, and righteousness will find you in proportion to your worship. Your worship will bring faith which will separate you from sin, an ever-present state of unrighteousness apart from Him.

41. Enjoying God Is Hardest for Those Who Enjoy Being Human.

*"Whom have I in heaven but you? And being
with you, I desire nothing on earth."*

—Psalms 73:25

Being human is an obstruction to enjoying God. Humanity does not prefer the concept of a *creator* because it overvalues itself. We loathe constraints. We forget our mortality for a time. We wrestle with our own graven images. Thus, our humanity separates us from God.

Enjoying God comes to those who seek him without ceasing. Those who seek God discover quickly how our stories begin and end. Our brief attempt at humanity between our beginning and our end shows us that faith precedes obedience. That faith must be solid enough to stand on, pliable enough to build on, and God-centered enough to keep on.

42. Situations Where Caring Is Warranted.

"Do to others as you would have them do to you."

—Luke 6:31

- You cannot care for someone more than they should care for themselves.
- Investments in caring must be rewarded, grown or written off.
- We are not called to wallow in the circumstances or attitudes of others.
- Caring is an art form, usually with no easy brush strokes.
- Caring is the struggle to know what to do, when to do it, and how to accept the results of trial and error.
- Caring requires the rational person to draw lines and limits.
- Disinvestment in one type of caring does not mean that you do not care.
- Good money and good caring that produce bad outcomes damage the pocketbook and the spirit.
- Too much inappropriate concern can lead to dependence, disrespect, or a bottomless pit.
- Caring is a combination of humility, understanding, adaptability, and considered direction.
- Learning and reproof must be imparted with care.
- We are called to be salt and light in the world, particularly a world that has little taste or vision.

43. Communication Is Much More than Talking about Situations.

> *"Jesus called the crowd to him and said, listen and understand."*
> —Matthew 15:10

- Words hold more meaning the deeper a relationship.
- The "gift of gab" is saying the most with the least gab about self.
- Listen for what is truly said, who is saying it, and why it is essential to prepare a situationally aware response.
- Words heard should ring true in the ear of the listener to create effective results.
- When two have talked more than enough, it is best to shut up.
- Discernment is dependent on both the speaker and the hearer.
- When the message and the messenger are wrong, the cost to make wrong right is substantial.

44. Words Bend Situational Understanding.

"Test everything. Hold on to the good. Avoid every kind of evil."

—1 Thessalonians 5:21-22

Words and actions based on fact add valuable understanding, whether free to be told or not. Words and actions based on emotions cause false reporting, unsubstantiated reactions, unreasonable consequences, and waste time and resources. Listen for what is said but also for what is unsaid, which can be more telling than what is said.

The Bible is replete with examples of word pictures and admonitions to the hearers of words and, specifically, of the need to speak of and listen to what is right and true. "Guard your mouth," "listen to God," "avoid the words of fools," "boast not," "behold what is good," "profit from words of rebuke," and "say only what is true" are Biblical admonitions by which to live.

Vanity is an undesired entrant into the word equation and mis-informs. It can color both speech and hearing to the point of destruction. In other words, speak the truth, speak with purpose, speak with concern, be genuine, and do not lose yourself in the sanctity of the words you speak when delivering a message. Again, be aware that unspoken words can convey a message of import.

45. Discernment Is an Essential Part of Awareness.

"The man without the Spirit does not accept the things that come from the Spirit of God, for they are foolishness to him, and he cannot understand them, because they are spiritually discerned."

—1 Corinthians 2:14

- Learning is not what one knows but knowing what is unknown and then discovering it.
- Tomorrow provides the discernment we lack today only if we strive to make it ours.
- People who rely on what they see or hear in the material world are trapped in a jaded world of expectations.
- Knowledge that leads to pride is not knowledge that leads to substance.
- Discern that which you should not do, in that which you are doing, and escape immediately.
- People who think they know what to look for in life risk seeing only a small number of trees in a very large forest.
- The foundation for discernment is knowing that every thought that enters the mind is either of God or absent God.

46. The Economics of One God Overwhelm the Economics of Many Gods.

"You believe that there is one God. Good! Even the demons believe that – and shudder."

—James 2:19

- Competition promotes innovation, efficiency, and lower costs in human endeavors but confuse those pursuing competing gods.
- Material and spiritual worlds war over the *one* God versus multiple definitions of a god.
- Man needs one firm foundation to enable him to sort through competing influences and interests.
- Sensuality and intellect are distractions from faith and hope in *one* God.
- Worshipping *one* God is far deeper and consequential than acknowledging many in season.
- Secular humanism leads the mind to loathe the idea that *one* God can judge sin and save sinners.
- *One* omnipresent, omnipotent, omniscient God has little use for gods created by men and women.

47.   God, Family, and Country Are Priorities for Every Situation.

"Blessed is the nation whose God is the Lord,
the people He chose for His inheritance."

—Psalms 33:12

- The "God/family/country" order is key to longevity and health, whether sought or wanted by individuals, families, or nations.
- Societies devalue "God/family/country" as men determine what is pure in their own eyes.
- Governments threaten the order and importance of faith in God and in families for power purposes.
- Cultural priorities for spending, for saving, and for God interfere with sound economics.
- The Puritan ethic at work in people has produced more economic advantage than sociopolitical engineering ever can.
- Ego is a most dangerous enemy of faith in God, family, and country.
- A built-in systemic justice impacts those who revere God or, alternatively, dismiss him.

48. Time Sensitive Situational Economics Are Always with Us.

"He said to them: It is not for you to know the times or dates the Father has set by his own authority."

—Acts 1:7

- Time heals, time destroys, and time marches on, but time itself influences yet does not takes sides in situations.
- Buyers and sellers must meet in agreement at the right time.
- Every man's timing is frail, but God's power is not time-restricted.
- A life's story is continually unfolding and remembered only for its use of time.
- Serving all the time improves one's economics in time.
- God provides in His own way, in His own time, knowing how to best use our limited time.
- We each play but one part in time yet fail to comprehend our influences over time.
- Pride interferes with the best use of time.
- Time-tested truths take time to be learned and applied by each generation.
- Time does not directly value successes and failures or even progress, but God does.

49. Naïvete Is an Awareness Affliction.

> *"For the time will come when men will not put up with sound doctrine. Instead, to suit their own desires, they will gather around them a great number of teachers to say what their itching ears want to hear. They will turn their ears away from truth and turn aside to myths."*
>
> —2 Timothy 4:3-4

- Innocence and unsophistication do not go unpunished.
- Evil takes advantage of the naïve, particularly those with deep pockets.
- Naïvete to the needs, plights, and secrets of others is an over-employed excuse.
- The noise that consumes our awareness fosters naïvete.
- Naïvete can lead to a little contentment or a lot of discontentment as the results come in.
- The naïve are rarely subtle in their misguidedness.
- Embracing big truths minimizes the consequences of naïve choices.
- The Bible admonishes those who would be naïve.
- God values wisdom, knowledge, and awareness in both theory and practice.
- Experience changes naïvete if only to produce circumspection.

50. Born-Again Awareness.

"You, dear children, are from God and have overcome them, because the one who is in you is greater than the one who is in the world."

—1 John 4:4

Powers of light and powers of dark affect the world whether we notice or not. Do you sense that your spirit is not alone in creation? Do you understand the ultimate choice you must make between God and Satan? Which of the two provides blessings, including life itself? Which of the two leads to regret? Which of the two provides shelter and comfort? Which of the two is light midst darkness? Given that perspective, know that the good deeds we do come from God just as the evil we do comes from us, courtesy of the great tempter. If you own that awareness, the Savior is building greatness in you.

51. God Thoughts for Every Situation.

"...being confident of this, that he who began a good work in you will carry it on to completion until the day of Christ Jesus."

—Philippians 1:6

- We demand more of God than God demands of us, yet He continues to supply more than we deserve to ask for.
- Blessings come to those who seek to know God before asking for the desires of the heart.
- Too little reverence for God leads to too little reverence for anything.
- If we do not fear God, we play God without knowing the plot or our role in it.
- Instant Christianity cannot be confined to an instant because faith is an ever-growing process.
- We can know God but may not be aware of God working in us and through us.

52. All Design Is for the Lord's Good Pleasure.

"Teach me to do your will, for you are my God;
may your good Spirit lead me on level ground."
—Psalms 143:10

- Man can never comprehend the fullness and reach of God's pleasure.
- It must be pleasing to God when we do what He admonished us to do.
- Christ did not please Himself but pleased the Father who sent Him.
- Honoring God, in whatever form, pleases him beyond our meager deeds.
- God takes no pleasure in the deaths or failures of unrepentant sinners.
- Riches and pleasures in life are but a temporary bonus for those who follow the Lord.
- Free will and forgiveness are inherent in God's good pleasure.
- God's good pleasure becomes more relevant to us the moment God becomes relevant to us.
- Prayer is a most conspicuous witness of our desire to please God.
- God's good pleasure is to be breathed in and received, not argued by narrow minds.
- God's good pleasure sustains those who seek sustenance and some who do not.
- God's grand design provides standards for man to prosper and please.
- God's good pleasure may, at times, vex, terrify, and sadden for a greater purpose.

53.   God Is *Not* the Source of Your Confusion.

*"The heart is deceitful above all things and
beyond cure. Who can understand it?"*
—Jeremiah 17:9

Economics, politics, peace, and attitudes change quickly
or slowly for better or worse. Both righteousness and evil spawn
gain and unjust gain, innovation and obsolescence, power and
weakness, wealth and poverty, diligence and surrender, progression
and regression, spirituality, and so many other human conditions.
Confusion is the by-product of too much speed in too wrong a
direction; yet, man rarely sees the confusion coming. When confusion
becomes intolerable, some men blame God.

Believers and nonbelievers experience confusion in every corner
of life. God never promised us a rose garden after the fall. Instead,
God has given man wisdom, commandments, counsel, understanding, courage, and integrity to combat the ills of confusion before,
during, and after they appear. Men and women are blessed with
abilities, insight, assets, a sense of timing, and modicum of wisdom
to combat trials and tribulations, not only to endure but also to
overcome. Temporary confusion in this life can, thereby, transition
into security, peace, stability, and joy. The economic value of confusion then lies in its eternal purpose, a purpose built to turn toward a
steady direction.

54. Situational Worry Does Not Improve Economics.

"Cast your cares on the Lord and he will sustain you; he will never let the righteous fall."
—Psalms 55:22

- Worry produces little positive return on investment.
- Worry leads to fear which often clouds opportunities.
- Worry hampers doing what needs to be done and when.
- Worry interferes with listening, objectivity, and speaking distinctively.
- Many needlessly worry about the wealth they possess and the wealth they want to possess.
- Worry sees the future bleakly, the present dimly, and the past regretfully.
- Today's worry will pass away in favor of a new worry unless faith enters in.
- Worry is a disease and thankfulness the cure.
- Worry often creates demands for which there is inadequate supply.

55. Practical Wisdom Revisited.

"The fruit of the righteous is a tree of life, and he who wins souls is wise."

—Proverbs 11:30

- Wisdom often appears in the dark, though the dark despises it.
- When caught between a heart and a mind in search of wisdom, look up.
- Wisdom is as much a matter of discipline as it is discernment.
- True wisdom will light up a life for others to see.
- Minds grow wiser when self grows smaller.
- Wisdom creates anticipation, action, and results.
- Wisdom knows that sin bleeds consequences, very often with no bandages.
- Good works are inherently good whether they work or not.
- Wisdom on earth matters to both those who seek it and to those who stray from it.
- Priorities are of the heart once the mind makes its contribution.
- Turning to God requires learning how God would have us turn.
- Promises made must be promises kept regardless of the economics or changes.
- Loosen your grip on things held too tightly, or you will lose your grip on more than things.
- The priorities of God prevent us from being hurt by our own.

56. The Jesus Power Brand Deserves Complete Awareness.

"I can do everything through him who strengthens me."

—Philippians 4:13

- Meek, not weak
- Asset without liability
- Teachings span eternity
- Courage beyond compare
- The Ultimate forecaster
- Reconciler
- Righteous beyond description
- Blameless
- Sharp and cutting truths
- All wisdom and knowledge
- Blots out sins and cancels debts
- Beginning and end of time and substance
- Multiplier for the faithful
- Never obsolete
- Lights the dark for the blind to see
- Creator and innovator
- No substitute
- Increases those who ask
- Unwavering rules that work
- Worth not calculable
- Merciful judge
- Wields the scepter of righteousness
- Fully man and fully God
- Timeless throne lasts forever

57. From God to Those Who Would Listen to His Inspired Word.

"I warn everyone who hears the words of the prophesy of this book: If anyone adds anything to them, God will add to him plagues described in this book."

—Revelation 22:18

- I formed you in my image.
- Walk in wisdom, speak truth, and do what is right.
- Rejoice always, pray without ceasing, and give thanks in all circumstances.
- Do not repay evil for evil but always seek to do good to one another.
- Hold fast to what is good, abstain from every form of evil.
- Prosperity and security are fleeting in man's existence.
- Admonish the idle, encourage the fainthearted, help the weak, and be patient with all.
- You are the sum product of your genetics, learning, your humility, and your receptivity to the Holy Spirit.
- Faithfulness calms the anxious.
- The discomfort of sin never eases without repentance.
- Death comes to all.

58. Sound Judgment Is Needed in Every Situation.

"But solid food is for the mature, who by constant use have trained themselves to distinguish good from evil."

—Hebrews 5:14

- "Judge not that ye be not judged" does not preclude good judgment.
- Never judge a book by its cover unless the cover is all that remains.
- Never judge a book by its author or you will be sorely disappointed.
- Guilt is determined by the guilty, not the guilt police.
- Doing what is judged right in our own eyes often proves the need for better eyeglasses.
- Morality and immortality are separate yet related in the final judgment.
- Avoid judges who judge for their own profit.
- The elephant in the room is often judged by repentance and forgiveness or an absence of either or both.
- Judgment is not sinful until it is.

59.   Be Aware of Unanticipated Detours in Our Great Race.

*"Enter through the narrow gate. For wide is the
gate and road is the road that leads to destruction,
and many enter through it."*

—Matthew 7:13

- Most detours in life are manmade and of little real importance.
- What we do not see along our way is cause for looking.
- Idols create detours the instant we permit them to become idols.
- Contemplating opposites reveals potential rocks and hard places ahead.
- Righteous behavior is infectious to all travelers.
- Life's big and little detours may lie hidden to the masses until they produce public crises.
- Truth brings freedom from life's potholes.
- Sleep hinders any race.
- You are the author of your *great race* but ask the Lord for His good speed.

60. Worldliness Overwhelms the Best of Situations.

"Avoid godless chatter, because those who indulge in it will become more and more ungodly."
—2 Timothy 2:16

- Anger is overwhelming while jealousy is destructive.
- Those who would diminish God in this world, diminish their abilities to cope.
- When you cannot see a way out, look beyond yourself and your limitations.
- When enough is enough, a complete transformation is not too much.
- A right theology makes the wrong happenings in life more bearable.
- Forgiveness is a choice that emotions often forestall.
- Evil is everywhere and cares not about sensible limits.
- "Group think" often overwhelms the minds of members who do not think.
- Panic overtakes those who expect more than true substance can offer.

61. Random Acts of Kindness and Industriousness Are Not Random.

> *"And we pray this in order that you may live a life worthy of the Lord and may please him in every way: bearing fruit in every good work, growing the knowledge of God."*
>
> —Colossians 1:10

- Responding to situations where kindness and industry are needed is a never-ending pastime.
- Actions are unpredictable until they become second nature and, therefore, not random.
- Pushing the envelope is good for you, for others, and for the envelope.
- Creation and recreation operate jointly unless one creates no room for the other.
- The intellect of the mind can harm the intelligence of the heart.
- Be wary of those who do good to look good.
- Not all acts are freely given or freely received.
- Counting wins and losses is not a measure of kindness nor industry.
- Kindness and industry contribute more to a situation than the immediate need.
- Man's institutions care less about kindness and industry than their own survival.
- A leap of faith is often required to be kind and industrious; the question is how high to leap.

62. The Economics of Love Require Keen Awareness.

"Because of the increase of wickedness, the love of most will grow cold, but he who stands firm until the end will be saved."
—Matthew 24:12-13

- Love is in greater demand than its human supply can provide.
- A single act of love multiplies as hearts pay it forward.
- Love never fails whether it is sufficient for the moment or not.
- Love possesses a unique blend of utility and comfort that often gets passed around.
- There is always someone on the opposite side of love.
- True love is never fully available without help from above.
- Real love makes the present moment a path for future moments.
- Christ's love does not reach a point of diminishing returns.
- Love invested often expects love in return which is why so many investments are written off.
- The mind muses about love while the heart takes a risk.
- Feeling love and speaking of love are different from willing and serving love.
- Think of His journey through hell the next time you confine Jesus's love to that of human love.
- God's love pursues every man and woman, but it is up to us to be caught.
- Love is lost when the lost cannot love.

63. New Creations Are Never Old.

"Therefore, we will not fear, though the earth gives way and the mountains fall into the heart of the sea…"

—Psalms 46:2

- Be willing to live two-standard deviations from where you now live comfortably.
- Comfort is a product of creation, not recreation.
- The greater the innovation, the greater the cost, time, and resistance.
- Money is always more limiting than imagination when creating.
- The freedom to innovate should not be taken for granted.
- The economics of discontent motivate only a few enough to change lives.
- An ideal end comes at the beginning of a new ideal objective.
- Old is only as old as you make it until the value of the old cannot be made anew.
- Doing your best is always best but not usually best for long or for all.
- The advantage of being first prospers only if first is not too early or too late.
- Static and dynamic are always out of sync.
- If the future is merely a linear extension of the past, there is little future in it.
- The things you ponder determine the things you will do something about.

In conclusion, a God-inspired spirit creates an opportunity-seeking mind to profit every situation. It is up to a man's spirit to see God's will in the situation.

II. Life Economics Awareness Is Artfully Scientific

"Whoever watches the wind will not plant; whoever looks at the clouds will not reap. As you do not know the path of the wind, or how the body is formed in a mother's womb, so you cannot understand the work of God, the Maker of all things. Sow your seed in the morning, and at evening let not your hands be idle, for you do not know which will succeed, whether this or that, or whether both will do equally well."

—Ecclesiastes 11:4-6

64. Economics 101: Six Pillars of Man's Economy

1. We learn economics, violate economics, and create economics every day.
2. Economics are ultimately about power and the discretionary use thereof.
3. Financial cycles are inevitable in man's economy as opportunity chases advantage until fear no longer sees it.
4. Supply never equals demand because anticipation constantly changes either the supply or the demand or both.
5. The innovative always find resources that non-resourceful people neglect, and profit is born.
6. Doing what is comfortable leads herds to follow trends long after trends cease to be trends.

65. Economics 201: Analysis Matters but Direction Matters More.

Return on investment, marginal utility, the velocity of money, debt loads, and inflation/deflation indicators are vital measures for financial success and sustainability in man's economy. The illusion that money, rather than functional utility, is most important can lead to speculations beyond reason. Financial limits are generally undefined or unheeded until forced.

Innovation is key to direction. Positive and negative incentives to innovate matter. Investment determines how much and how quickly innovation proceeds. Cost control, credit availability, and human initiative are deciding factors in anything new. With innovation, mistakes are made. Losses may be taken. Governments may regulate beyond reason. Macroeconomic deterrents happen. Businesses may close. Changes usually happen prior to predictions. People fail in economic and noneconomic ways. It is important to be aware that a constant battle exists between the status quo and the profitability of anything new. Satisfaction with what exists, barriers to entry in established markets, advantages accruing to the incumbents, knowledge gaps, creditworthiness, taxes, and market psychology can slow innovation. Barriers pass away, and all things worthy of becoming new become new. One viable idea is all it takes.

66. Value Lies in the Person and the Persona in Each Situation.

- Value represents the importance we give to anything or anyone until we find something or someone more valuable.
- Value exists solely in the eye of the beholder until friendly and unfriendly beholders impact what the eye sees.
- The real value of anything equals the cost of not having it, especially when we need it.
- People who speculate about value are often blind to their own speculation until it is obvious.
- People and things neither attain nor retain their highest and best value for long in situations.
- Value is subject to an ever-changing score kept on an economic scoreboard that constantly changes.
- A person may need to adapt his or her persona to change situations.
- Human values may last a lifetime but do not register in eternity.
- God values situational righteousness above all else.

67. Business Realities for Every Situation.

- Make the complex simple for many to use efficiently and the economics will work.
- Begin with enough capital to survive the first year's learning curve.
- Hire an accountant who knows how to count.
- Customers who do not pay on a timely basis cannot be customers over time.
- Seek customer feedback from *day one* and take it to heart.
- Sales and profit margin changes reveal a profitable future or death by obsolescence.
- Partners need early agreement on what it takes to be a partner in changing situations.
- The mind of an entrepreneur is wired to create but not necessarily to account.
- Being an entrepreneur is not for everyone; being an underfunded entrepreneur is for no one.
- Opportunity lies in knowing how the cost of something changes the costs of other things.
- Obsolescence is more real to those whose career or business is obsolete or becoming so.
- Examine the features, benefits, and flaws of anything to build a better mousetrap.
- Automating the usual is good; creating the unusual is better.
- Draw lines to measure progress early in the innovation process.
- Entrepreneurs always have a better idea tomorrow.
- Keep an ever-vigilant eye on the competition for they will not go quietly into oblivion.
- If at first you don't succeed, there is always a missing key that will open a closed door.
- Encouragement from within and a lot of prayer is needed for those who take risks.

68. Rational and Intuitive Economic Choices Arise Daily.

Good economic decisions require information, experience, and known objectives. Fact or experience-based choices may be made by numbers alone; however, intuition creeps into the decision-making process and can overwhelm the numbers. Past results can anchor the assumptions upon which both good and bad decisions are made. On the other hand, good and bad feelings about a situation and the parties involved should be taken seriously.

In business and personal affairs, economics ultimately rule. Profits keep the lights on. When profits do not exist or when the number of options is limited, decisions must force change. Hard questions must be asked and answered quickly. Routine discussions of options promote the much advertised out-of-the-box thinking. Past deceptions should become increasingly obvious. As the availability or the nonavailability of options become a daily subject of discussion, the status quo loses its attractiveness.

Take a hard look at the opposite of what you are doing or thinking. Rid your mind of bias, stale information and emotional attachments as you highlight obsolete assumptions. An assumed strength can be a real weakness while a weakness can serve as the foundation for a redesigned strength.

69. Investing is Both an Art and a Science Plus a Lot of Luck.

- Learning how to accurately keep score is the first step to keeping the score within boundaries.
- It is better to learn about finances before you learn finances from personal loss.
- Do not assume that past investment performances guarantee the future.
- Learn to go with a strong current in whatever you do while keeping a keen eye on opportunities to get out of the water.
- Irrational exuberance is more about being rational than exuberant.
- Dependable profits are key to portfolio investments only if truly dependable.
- Politics interfere with investments when those investments are not profitable for politicians.
- Diversification is good in rising tides but are just as subject to sinking in rough seas.

70. A Money Plan Should Prepare for the Worst and the Best While Being Content in the Situations in Between.

- Money can be a blessing or a battleground, determined by hearts who have it and those who want it.
- Money comes with foresight and commitment but departs with excess spending and risk.
- In the worst of times, know that the assets others know you own are coveted, especially when they need them.
- In any time, know that future pay raises for your job are possible only if that job has a future.
- In good and bad times, know that the more we have, the more we want, if we fail to realize how much we have been given to give.
- Some worry more about money when they have it than those who do not.
- Contentment is more in our control than the things and people beyond our control.
- Sustainability is the primary issue in personal money matters, particularly when the sustainability of others may be your risk.
- Save more than you think, spend less than you want, and invest in people and things that last.
- Expected returns on investments may change markedly and all too quickly.

71. Investment Requires Money and More than Money Awareness.

Investment in money assets usually requires investment in people. Someone must write the operations manual and that someone must know the numbers, including the present value of the investment as it relates to the future probabilities of actual returns. That someone must also prove trustworthy in reporting results, seeing current and future options, and, generally, showing good horse sense regarding the economic times.

Investment in people is much the same. People can produce great returns or may become a giant sucking sound. Societal benevolence, meanwhile, can be tolerated only until an economic profit should be expected from each person involved. Avoid those who would spend more time and effort soliciting more from you and others than focusing on the details of the enterprise in place.

72. We Take Risk and Avoid Risk and Often Fail to Understand it.

- Great risks arise when little risks are disregarded for too great a time.
- A riskless life is for dead minds and lazy souls.
- Life preservers are often too big, too small, too neglected, or lost.
- Risk is never fully understood until it becomes personal.
- A risk that can be controlled is not a risk that prevents sleep or empties the pocketbook.
- Know your risk tolerance and the costs for risk avoidance.
- Go into the world; the risk you take is often better than waiting for the world to come to you.
- The greatest risk we bear comes from not aligning our lives with God.

73. Is Your Job Situation at Risk?

- If you are the highest paid, those who maximize profits will target you.
- Entry level jobs are the easiest to automate.
- If you make yourself nonessential, why would anyone consider you essential?
- Your strengths and weaknesses always define your employability.
- Industries and jobs come and go faster than routine employees anticipate.
- New and old competitors determine how much fat your company must lose.
- Profit margins are the best indicator of where you will end up.
- Paying attention to more than the weekend will give you a sense of impending risks.

74. There Is Power and Profit in Serving.

- Profits come to those who serve and satisfy the needs and wants of others.
- Waiting for the rewards of service may take more time than anticipated.
- Serving is an attitude and an aptitude grounded in humility.
- Self-control is a requisite in serving.
- Commitment to greater than oneself minimizes the temptation to stray from the mission.
- Serving will be honored by others but a healthy or unhealthy dependence often results.
- A serving spirit disarms powers, authorities, and deceivers.
- Your model of service can build character in others.
- Serving need not require suffering.
- Lost relationships can be redeemed in service, even if one side remains lost.
- The ultimate objective of service is God saying, "Well done, my good and faithful servant."

75.   Profits Are More About Cost Control than Selling Price.

Controlling the cost of anything increases the likelihood selling that anything will be profitable. The more variable a cost, the less likely it can be controlled. If possible, transfer your variable costs to those who are better able to ensure that those costs remain fixed for you. As a rule, people costs vary more than equipment or technology costs. Insuring costs for the long run may require investment which could add cost in the short run.

Check every day on your suppliers and your competition. Their situations can determine your future. Locate better sources of supply and products that could serve as substitutes. One of the greatest risks in any situation is getting paid for credit extended which affects to your ability to pay those you owe. The everyday goal is to create and maintain adequate profit margins. Note that profits in spiritual matters are also cost-sensitive.

Random Business Cost Paranoia

- Relationships can be costly, particularly if agreements favor the other side from the outset.
- Franchise models limit the unknowns but only some of the mistakes of unwary franchisees.
- Take or pay contracts usually lower cost but are best when confident of the amounts needed.
- Savvy creditors demand personal asset guarantees which may cost dearly.
- Variable interest rates go down slowly but can bust a budget when quickly on the rise.
- Ordinary costs and extraordinary costs are too often extraordinary.
- The ideal cost is the one on which profit is not vitally dependent.

76. Balance Is a Situational Asset.

- Balance is the key to our individual and collective situations.
- Balance in pride versus humility creates attitude. Balance in integrity versus desire creates character.
- Balance in guidance versus freedom creates stability.
- Balance in investing versus hoarding creates industry.
- Balance in work versus idleness creates prosperity.
- Balance in power versus meekness creates leadership.
- As has been mentioned, balance flows into imbalance unless imbalance is counteracted quickly. Assets and liabilities have a way of reversing themselves. Note that righteousness is an asset that may require change; however, it is never out of date.

77. Carrots and Sticks Nudge Choices.

Incentives and disincentives abound in life, some naturally, some by intent, and some by accident. Self-interest selects between incentives and the disincentives, the necessary and the unnecessary, the profitable and that which only looks profitable, the pain versus the gain, the promised and the real, the freedom to choose versus the obligation to choose, risk versus safety, an iron hand versus gentle prodding, the end game versus present advantages, and many other qualitative and quantitative trade-offs.

Everyone gives and receives carrots or sticks over a lifetime. There are real trade-offs between carrots and sticks and real consequences, particularly if there are too many carrots or too few sticks.

The role of carrots and sticks is simple. We are to take honest advantage of every carrot and guard against being hit by every stick. Be aware that many carrots and sticks come in disguise.

78. Manias Mix Mental Health with Finances.

In psychology, the words used to describe a mania include abnormal arousal, excitement, delusion, excess enthusiasm, over activity, and mental illness. The term manic depression points to the uncontrollability of up and down mood swings.

In the world of finance, manias are born when investors chase the same or similar investments with dreams of riches in increasingly popular assets such as land, stocks, gold, or tulip bulbs. During manias, feelings of greed and fear (not facts) rule herds of investors who cannot discriminate between the two. Exuberance has a way of chasing hot trends long after the trends cease to be trends. The speculation, in its later stages, becomes a disease of the intellect, of the spirit and of finances.

Manias end when enough people recognize that what has been chased is becoming worth less, bordering on worthless. As everyone rushes to be first out of the boat, fear of loss sets in. For those who were not able to find the exit or a lifeboat, depression sets in, followed by economic depression.

Asset manias run in cycles, existing whether we see them or not. Stock momentum traders chase newly popular assets, not on intrinsic value, by chasing movement swings up and down. Mania result with too much movement in either direction. We are likely facing the tumultuous end of the greatest financial/economic mania in recorded history because of a debt bubble. If you sense that mania or any mania, secure a lifeboat!

79. Timing Is Everything for Every Situation.

- There is a time to maximize what you have and a time to minimize what may be taken away.
- The time to exit gracefully is when sustainability is predictable, one way or the other.
- Each season has a beginning and an end with an enterprise in between.
- Unusual things happen in their own time, particularly when we fail to recognize the times.
- Time on earth is easy to abuse when we think ourselves to be masters of our times.
- Our race against time is measured by our speed, our endurance, and the tick of the time clock.
- There is a time to simplify affairs, both for yourself and your heirs.
- Timing is the foundation upon which the creations of men are built and destroyed.
- God has His own timing despite efforts of men to predict it, refute it, or change it.

80. Indebtedness Is a Consuming Condition.

- Debt is a burden created by overindulgence and over-zealousness.
- A sea of debt teaches the rich and the poor how to swim or get out of the water.
- Legal remedies do not take the place of the moral requisites of debt repayment.
- In times of easy credit, incentives to borrow consumes the rich and the poor.
- Incurring debt is a matter of the spirit; money simply follows in lockstep.
- If you lend, get rock solid collateral to guarantee repayment.
- The less you owe, the more control you have over what you owe.
- The more you owe, the more control those you owe have over you.
- The greatest debt we owe is not of money but of the sins of our souls.

81. Big Versus Little Is a Constant Battle.

- The bigger an organization, the more fragile its continuance.
- Vacuums in leadership, purpose and sensibility flourish with larger size.
- Little is generally more efficient than big unless big can purchase more at lower cost.
- Correcting correctable parts is easier with little if corrections are not too big.
- Benevolence to a few is easier to police than benevolence to many, especially with governments.
- Big vision is better than little vision even regarding little issues.
- A single heart is easier to save than a collective heart, which is why God views us one by one.
- The problem with little is that it often gets big while the problem with big is its resistance to becoming efficiently little.

82. Spending and Expending Are Critical to the Economics of Life.

- Spending is a habit, an addiction that can be overcome with habitual saving.
- Know that a next purchase influences the purchase after that.
- Those with the least who give the most are more satisfied than those with the most who give the least.
- The more moving parts you die with, the harder it is for others to keep them moving.
- The more freedoms you create for others, the greater the rewards for others and you.
- Generations rise and fall according to the spending habits of previous generations.
- Expending is commitment to purpose while spending may have a purpose without commitment.

83. Wise Advice for Kids and Adults for Every Situation.

- Learn about finances long before finances teach you the hard way.
- Determine whether you are best being a leader or a follower and be the best.
- Educate yourself early and often, even if others dismiss the importance.
- The next book you read is worth far more than your next tweet or text.
- Find true friends who are tactful friends of the unvarnished truth.
- Minds grow wiser when they put self in a faraway place.
- Forgive yourself and others for the troubles in life.
- As hormones rage, emotions control the ability to think and discern.
- Reputations are made and lost by conspicuous words and deeds repeated for cause.

84. Real Estate Is a Fixed Situation.

Real estate is ownable, habitable, rentable, fixed in location, financeable, costly to maintain, and generally considered a prime investment. One investment in real estate is enough for most people, but more is usually considered better absent too much debt. All real estate appreciates and depreciates due to physical and situational economic forces. Appreciation is appreciated far more than depreciation.

The credit available to purchasers, including investors, determines the demand for real estate which, in turn, determines its value. Credit booms create real estate booms while credit busts create real estate busts. Being fixed on location adds measurably to the boom or bust of a neighborhood or a nation. Thus, real is real when the estate remains useful and financeable and painfully real when we are in debt and can no longer afford it.

Appraise the real estate you have or want and do not take it for granted. Obsolescence may creep up on you or happen quickly, physically or economically. As an example, shopping malls, once a very profitable real estate investment, are currently experiencing less retail traffic and less solvent retail tenants. Debt load risk forces stable rents (and values) to become less stable. Unlike mobile assets, moving a shopping mall to greener pastures is not an option.

85. Economic Righteousness Is Hard to Define, Let Alone Practice.

People demand and people supply and the balance between the two is ever-changing. Christians, and those critical of Christians, often assume that loving your neighbor means everyone should have access to essentials. But to make that access possible, people must work and work smartly and efficiently to afford the access. Somewhere in that work is righteousness. Without work, economics cannot work. Without righteousness, work loses its real worth.

A greater good (aka righteousness) is not greater if it is not greater for many. However, a greater good is not always guaranteed in life. Decisions to work, to create, or to invest are not always rewarded.

Some argue that a person's decision to work or not should not be the sole deciding factor in personal economics while others argue that each person should be responsible for his or her own decisions and the associated results. Both sides seek a greater good, but the greatest righteousness that man can create lies in creating the greatest number of free choices for themselves and others, including the opportunity to work. Behind the scenes, God's *Invisible Hand* helps those who help Him by helping themselves but not exclusively.

86. Practical Economics Under God.

- Practical is what works successfully; perfect is not practical in man's economy.
- Wealth is defined by the matters of the spirit and physical tangibles held closely.
- A fifty-year Biblical Jubilee practice constrains melt ups and melt downs.
- Obedience to God leads to prosperity while destruction comes from rebellion.
- Preparedness in good times saves enough to survive lean times.
- Economies of scale disappear as quickly as they come.
- Currencies were minted intermittently with varied successes in empires now gone.
- The process of *creative destruction* in spiritual and material economics is apparent throughout history, uniquely in Noah's time.
- Bartering has been a historical part of life with tangibles assets and services.
- Local and national taxes and tax collectors maintain a hated public treasury, unless used efficiently.
- Covetousness dooms many, particularly those who flaunt their wealth.
- Sowing and reaping are inescapable corollaries.
- Talents buried are opportunities lost.
- Do not borrow against your chickens before they hatch.
- Seasons come and go inside and outside of your personal economic circles.
- Wealth is often carried off in the night by a foreign or local power.
- You next meal is more important than all the mansions you may own.
- Change is not welcomed in any age; progress is essential in all ages but is not always enough.

- Have a back-up plan at the beginning for, by the end, promises and plans will change markedly.
- The heart and the pocketbook are both fickle.
- Those in power want to stay in power by taking whatever they can from the easiest source.
- False truths lead to speculation which end up in unrealizable expectations.
- There are two in you who are always in conflict about saving or spending money.
- Workers deserve to idle for a time but do not employ idlers who work for a short time.
- Investing in the Lord helps to better invest in people and things.
- Godliness is not a gambit; it holds a guarantee.
- Money is only as good as the person who has it and the government who backs it.
- A medium of exchange varies with time and circumstances and macroeconomics.
- Each personal economy has been divinely ordered.
- Money is never enough to overcome discontent.
- Value lies in being effective for an eternal purpose.
- The quintessential economic question is: "What belongs to me, and what belongs to God?"
- God's *laws of utility* are far different than man's values of materiality.
- Partnering with the Holy Spirit yields greater than hoped for profit.
- When we do not get what we want, perhaps there is something better we should want.
- God's agenda is often unseen, misunderstood, or different for those who cling to their own.
- Repentance changes spiritual and material economics.
- Fake economics proffer the same waste and destruction as fake information.
- Few would prefer receiving what they deserve.

- Finding happiness in riches or in poverty is not enough to create joy.
- Follow the money and you will see the heart leading.
- "I am that I am" is the rule that makes all other economic principles pale in comparison.
- Governments who play god do not advantage anyone but themselves.
- Robbing the poor appears in many forms and fashions: taxes, dependency, prices, supplies, and justice to name a few.
- Markets decide what is of value; God decides who is valuable and for what.
- Economic behavior is dictated by observation, learning, self-interest, and resolve.
- Altruism can motivate, but not all altruism is truth beyond questioning.
- Economic relationships among people and systems cannot breathe in a vacuum.
- No amount of behavioral economic control can guarantee that people will expend equally, act in unison, optimize in performing, or even behave.
- The strong remain fiscally strong by living within limits; the weak find their limits all too soon.
- The amount of money in an economy means little to those trapped in poverty.

87. Net Worth Is But a Number Representing a Moving Target.

Worthiness is a target never reached apart from God's grace. Nowhere is that more evident than with money. We continually earn or spend more than we earn or spend. Net worth in money terms is never constant nor ever worthy. Personal worth is similar; our self-worth and our worth to others is never constant. Our actions and reactions add to or subtract from that worth. Fortunately, *salvation* is not conditioned on our perceived worthiness for we are unworthy. Grace redeems the unworthiest among us if we but ask.

88. Retirement Funds Need More Money Coming In than Going Out.

Pension funds and insurance policies need approximately 8 percent annual returns on invested capital to stay solvent. They can, however, live with a lower rate of return for a short time, but the risks to pensioners of a promised benefit stream grow every moment that the necessary rate of return is not earned. Insurance policies also remain solvent by earning more than is paid out. If investment portfolios fall short of expected returns long enough, benefits may be reduced, even curtailed, or premiums may be raised when core capital is depleted. Credit unions, mortgage insurers, bond funds, and other retirement or benefit schemes are subject to the same economics. The Social Security System is not immune. Bottom line, more must come in than go out.

Now is the time to find out if your fund has over or under-performed. Be aware of false reporting. Seek options early if solvency appears to be an issue. Save separately from the plan at risk. Lower your expected pension living costs where possible. Consider not inputting more money if that money looks to you as investing good money after bad. Check with independent credit analysts for recommended investments that have a future. Always be involved in managing your own finances.

89. Leadership Changes the Economics of Any Situation.

- How leaders lead shapes, in part, how the led lead others.
- Good advice often results in the distribution of good advice.
- Parents lead generations by emphasizing God's word and its applications.
- Leaders who grasp fundamental economics find a hidden order that works.
- Herds wander aimlessly until a leader emerges to show a safe or a perilous way.
- The Lord gives power to those who lead for a little time and a higher purpose.
- God leads man to the simple, leaving the complex for himself.
- Turbulent times require leaders to offer specific hope to put at ease uneasy followers.

90. Never Give Up!

When chaos is all around, when friends and foes know not what to do, take a moment to give thanks for what you have, for what you understand, and for what you know that you do not understand. Then pray for wisdom, pray for strength, and pray for direction. The noise will quiet. The options will become clearer. Whether others follow or not, never become weary of doing good in chaos for good is what will distinguish you from the chaotic. Know that the best of discoveries take birth in the worst of times. Never tire of overcoming. *Never* give in or give up in any situation!

> "But as for you, be strong and do not give up, for your work will be rewarded."
> —2 Chronicles 15:7

In conclusion, a God-inspired spirit changes the economics at work for one and more than one in every situation.

III. Macroeconomic and Political Awareness: The Proximate and the Remote Are Intertwined for Better and for Worse— Yesterday, Today and Tomorrow

"The rich rule over the poor, and the borrower is servant to the lender."

—Proverbs 22:7

"When you reap the harvest of your land, do not reap the very edges of your field or gather the gleanings of your harvest. Leave them for the poor and the alien. I am the Lord your God."

—Leviticus 23:22

"Be sure to know the condition of your flocks, give careful attention to your herds, for riches do not endure forever, and a crown is not secure for all generations."

—Proverbs 27:23-24

"For our struggle is not against flesh and blood, but against the rulers, against the authorities, against the powers of this dark world and against the spiritual forces of evil in the heavenly realms."

—Ephesians 6:12

Mankind needs to be governed, yet man needs to be free. God calls us to submit to honorable government, certainly aware that governments are imperfect. Governments create darkness in economic, moral, and political affairs when God is neglected in the policy-making. Banning God from public places is an indication of how far a nation has travelled from our Creator.

People, for their part, demand unreasonable largesse from government. Special interests demand that their interests be served at the expense of others. Government, desiring to maintain power, grows to the point of suffocation from its own weight. Political and economic chaos is the eventual end as unsustainable debt, war, lawlessness, and unholy passions spread across societies. These are the worldwide times in which we live. Mankind now faces a significant turning. God has warned that, in such times, many untruths will become truths and confusion will reign. He admonishes us to be acutely aware in our comings and in our goings. The health of our bodies and our souls will depend on our preparations.

91.   The Time Has Come to Talk of Serious Limitations.

Democracies can be both a blessing and a curse. Few democracies maintain a lasting economic course, and the people are the reason why. The blessing is that people vote. The curse is that people vote. People vote their first vote and feel empowered by their freedom to vote. People often vote ensuing votes with their pocketbooks in mind. When enough people vote to take from the public treasury for themselves, or even for enough altruistic causes at the expense of solvency, the horn of plenty runs dry. Blessings taken for granted may then disappear in stages or all at once. A return to solvency is long and arduous even in the best of nations.

92. Sovereign Fragility Is Always the Situation.

- National, local, and personal debt destroys economic peace at its core.
- Nation states, mired in foreign wars, deplete a treasury beyond sustainability.
- Increasing the quantity of money in an economy through means other than profits destabilizes currencies.
- The next dollar spent by any government should create more than a dollar.
- Fiat currencies are a tool of the powerful used to bumfuzzle rich and poor.
- When citizens lose confidence in sovereigns, they choose private assets in which to hide.
- When the majority takes from a productive minority, the incentive to produce disappears.
- Covetousness ends in fragility for all concerned.
- Because of the ripple effects on lenders, economic mercy (aka legal bankruptcy) cannot become a routine debt forgiveness mechanism.

93. The Bigger the Technology, the Bigger the Risks.

Technology is a blessing when it works. Just-in-time delivery systems depend and on it. Mass communications air on it. Medical treatments thrive on it. Technology improves societal economics. But technology can be a god of confusion. The more dependence, the greater the chance of chaos. If one part of a system malfunctions, the whole system is in jeopardy as are its users. Reliance breeds both core and connected risks. When systems break down, the natural response is to turn to any means to obtain necessities, including violence.

Pundits and preppers have been both praised and ridiculed for forecasting systemic breakdowns of technology. Risk avoidance due to fear of loss is common sense in such times. Redundancy for critical systems becomes a risk worth taking for those concerned about potential natural or criminal interruption of essential services.

94.   Government Lacks a Soul and, Therefore, Accountability.

The temptations associated with power increase with time. Governments in distant places become tempted to rule according to the economics of those distant places, taking advantage of those they can. A public treasury then becomes a resource for personal treasure. Elites pass rules that expand advantages for themselves with decreasing accountability because the Deep State does not possess a conscience, a higher moral authority, or even a soul. It is as if the economic (and moral) lifeblood of governance is sucked out by parasites. Voters are, in theory, the higher power in governance; however, voters usually have a choice only among similar officialdoms. Accounting is, therefore, fostered only by limiting the time of their rule.

95.   The Distance an Empire Is from Its Godly Roots Equals the Time It Has Remaining.

Empires have been built and destroyed by force and by economic advantage. The greater the empire, the greater the number of special interests that arise in pursuit of power and wealth. The number and type of pursuits continue to rise until economics can no longer support them. When gaming a system becomes a way of life for special interests, history shows that the game is up.

There is a critical point where turning back to godly roots by a few is not enough to span the distance from God the many have travelled. Deaths of empires happen more slowly than quickly, absent a single terminal event. For Christians who think our times to be the *end-times*, note that several empires have disappeared over the last 2000 years, and the Second Coming of Christ did not occur as many in their time had anticipated. Jesus will certainly come again whenever He chooses, but He instructs followers to draw ever closer to God in all times.

96. Be Aware of the Lifestyles That Bind Us.

- Lifestyle is a series of choices that depend on motivation, income, and expending.
- Nations have a lifestyle too, dependent on motivation, income, and expectations.
- The availability of credit is a lifestyle financier.
- Governments tax and incur debt to maintain lifestyles and votes.
- Faith in government is a requisite for faith in lifestyle.
- Wars and debt crises cause life itself to be more important than lifestyle.
- Lifestyle cycles happen coincident with societal security.

As the prophet said, "There is a time for everything, and a season for every activity under heaven, a time to be born and a time to die, a time to plant and a time to uproot, a time to kill and a time to heal, a time to tear down and a time to build..."

—Ecclesiastes 3:1-3

97. Currencies Are Fiats; Fiats Stand for Something or Often Nothing.

Currencies are symbols of the governments, banks, or people who issue them. No currency, like no government, bank, or people, has proven dependable over history. When a fiat currency stands for less than promised (and the world knows it or even suspects it), panic begins.

Fiat currencies are meant to fool some of the people some of the time; however, most are fooled most of the time until an inflection point is reached. When obvious inflation or deflation set in, a new currency order is already under way. The assumed store of value has become tainted. The once trustworthy no longer deserves to be trusted. Minds then turn to other stores of value. In simple terms, a dollar is worth a dollar (even a devalued dollar) until faith in that dollar turns into fear that the standard is no longer the standard.

Currency threats are created by both national and international policy diseases, including artificial manipulations to maintain peaceful expected values. Too much debt, too little profit from trade, too little industry, too many taxes, and too many unbalanced budgets weaken fiat currencies to the point where rebalancing acts become futile. Nations that peg their currencies to other nations' currencies for stability sake need be constantly aware of misguided faith in those other nations and currencies. Even the best of a bad bunch of currencies has a limited life. Since currency values represent purchasing power, be aware and beware!

98. Woe to Wicked Nations and Peoples.

- Just as industry multiplies, so too does evil.
- The spirit of men mines or undermines ideas, intent, abilities, diligence, and finances.
- Gain and unjust gain deceive the best of us in the best and worst of nations.
- Godless peoples serve themselves while headed to oblivion.
- The wicked plot evil, spread strife, reject correction, and pervert even a little righteousness.
- With no spiritual restraint, citizen demands crush the best of nations.
- Wicked nations will know when the Holy Spirit finds them.
- Good and evil are every bit as fragile as the human heart.
- Evil comes in many forms, none without anguish.
- Ironically, the power to oppress oppresses both slaves and their masters.
- The demand for evil rarely exceeds its supply.

99. Symptoms of Evil in Jeremiah's Time and Our Own.

- God is increasingly disregarded and disdained.
- Innocent blood is shed.
- Deceptive words prevail as truth perishes.
- Discipline is absent; self-control is out of control.
- Everyone turns to his own course, rationalizing that right is wrong and wrong is right.
- Wisdom is shallow, devoid of God.
- There is no shame in abominations.
- Many pursue personal and societal idols.
- Evil becomes stronger than faith.
- Both the least and the greatest seek gain, often unjust gain.
- Joy cannot be found in the people.

100. Ezekiel 22 on Biblical Israel, Sound and Feel Familiar?

- Disregarded God's sabbaths
- Not taught the difference between clean and unclean
- No distinction between the holy and the common, exalting that which should not be exalted.
- Seeing false visions and divining lies for them
- A city (nation) that makes idols to defile herself
- Ruined human lives
- Priests perverted God's law
- Rulers destroy lives to get dishonest gain, oppressing the poor and needy
- Robbery, bribes, bloodshed, lewdness, turmoil

God's answer then was, "So I will pour out my wrath on them and consume them with my fiery anger, bringing down on their own heads all that they have done, declares the Sovereign Lord."

—Ezekiel 22:31

101. The Year of Jubilee: God's Way of Controlling the Situation.

The Year of Jubilee in ancient Israel was a God-ordained time of freedom and celebration. It occurred in the fiftieth year after seven sets of seven-year Shemitah cycles. It was a time of atonement, debts were forgiven, slaves were freed, land was returned to previous owners and the land laid fallow. A warning was issued to Israel if it failed to practice Jubilee, one of which was being scattered among the nations.

The Year of Jubilee and its tenets has not been celebrated consistently in modern times despite evidence of seven-year cycles in nature and economics. Atonement, debt forgiveness, slave freeing, and land reversion have been ordered by man in his own way apart from God. The result is systemic disequilibrium. The likelihood is that admonitions for a prescribed Year of Jubilee will be enforced if not pursued voluntarily.

The earthly calendar suggests that we are in or near a Year of Jubilee. The rules should be honored. But today's public and private debts are at record levels and increasing. Borrowing is well beyond the ability to repay. A create-new-debt-to-pay-back-old-debt mentality is in force to kick the can down the road. Innovative ways to cancel debt without repayment are being explored. Governments have repeatedly stepped in behind the scenes to backstop credit freezes and to control unsustainable liquidations.

God's *Invisible Hand* knows when too much is too much, hence the original rules and their cyclical timing. As national and international debts are liquidated, personal pocketbooks will be moth-eaten. God followers can only control what they can control but should take stock of assets and liabilities in light of Shemitah and Jubilee Year admonitions. Be prudent in all things, seek utility, return to the Lord as He would lead, and pray for wisdom. We are indeed free to choose our next path but be aware that all paths are littered with excesses.

102. Godless Societies Are Crushed by Their Own Designs.

- The rule of law is not a normal human condition.
- A dependable, predictable rule of law lessens the risk of taking risk.
- Economic growth happens when investment in tomorrow is legally encouraged.
- Powerful men are rarely satisfied with their own laws and, certainly, not God's laws.
- Liberty is built on a principled rule of law and lasts until lawlessness is not punished.
- Morals and ethics lead to laws based on justice and righteousness; without them, laws are unbinding or unenforced or both.
- Sentimentality too often impacts the disposition of a law.
- A heart for rule-keeping is more than simple obedience and disobedience to Caesar.

103. Human Legalism Fails Without Fail.

- Legal is not always moral or true.
- Illegal matters only when legal matters; immoral matters only when moral matters.
- Law enforcement can be legal and illegal at the same time.
- Legal rights are always subject to whims of government or the proletariat.
- Society determines what to defend, yet truth may drift with the wind.
- Neither equal rights nor equal opportunity under the law are equal in real life.
- Human legalism is but a poor substitute for God's perfect judgment.

104. Information Enables, Misinformation Disables, and Disinformation Destroys Truth.

False narratives cloud the truth and diminish the quest for truth. False narratives become mainstream when the mainstream seeks to further profit from that which is false. Mass media enables false narratives to appear true as gossipers perfect their craft. Facts become biased beyond recognition, raising doubts about sources in the minds of hearers to unintended higher levels. False facts follow under speciously created rules of disinformation.

The disappearance of truth through misinformation and disinformation breeds corruption. Corruption lies in all of us, and our communications evidence our levels of conscious or unconscious participation. Corrupt people use untruths to create corrupt economics which become economic only for the corrupt. Dishonesties multiply with increasing dishonesty for dishonest purposes. Group and institutional dishonesty spreads throughout a society seeking economic advantage. Even if we repent and correct untruths, civil and economic damage has been done.

One premise holds that the corrupt end up being defeated by their own corruption. It is the reaping and sowing concept applied to evil. It would be more than ironic if the corrupt are destined to be surrounded by the spiritual and material economics of their corruption for eternity. Idols sought on earth, including those of corrupt making, would surround the idolater in hell forever, a most unpleasant end.

105. War Is Always on the Horizon.

War is primarily about the power of economics or religion. Wealth is a target of aggressors. Others want what some have. Some nations try to produce or reproduce the means for wealth; others try to conquer it, but conquering has accompanying consequences for both the conqueror and the conquered. Winners think they have total victory until they must assimilate what they have won. Losers always lose something, if not everything.

Tax wars and trade wars are good examples of economic war. Taxes raise money for government in the short-term but reduce the incentive to invest. When less is available to be taxed, governments seek taxes from previously non-taxed sources, incentivizing producers to flee. Countries offering better competitive advantages win until the loser puts tariff taxes or fees on incoming goods to level the playing field and trade wars begin. Likewise, capital seeks advantage, fleeing uncertainty, chaos, projected war, and disincentives. Capital flows toward the greatest return on principal and/or the greatest safety of principal. Safety is not inherent in war, and whatever the impetus for war, capital is used up in noneconomic ways or invested in assets that hold value as far from the conflict as possible. Macroeconomically and politically aware people are the first to take flight as physical and economic safety become a top priority.

Within a nation, the war cycle between the haves and the have nots begins with a societal celebration for exceptional producers and a lauding of their achievements that have benefitted all. But as government hungers for more tax revenues from the prosperous, society turns and targets the exceptional. Wars on producers within a society always end badly. Less investment results in stale economics. As mentioned, disincentives send producers to other venues, states, or nations to produce. In addition, economic war often spills over into armed conflict, a boon for military economics but not so good for peaceful economics. Resources are wasted on destruction. Recovery takes a decade or two, depending on the freedoms, incentives, and credit available for rebuilding efforts.

Religious wars have similar consequences for similar reasons. Internal and external religious zealotry cost dearly. Internal and external political marriages between religious zealots and political powers cost freedoms. Meanwhile, religious movements often spill over into armed conflict, end destructively and cost lives and treasuries. Winners either impose their religions on others or spend decades recovering.

On the positive side, for those unaware of the causes of war, the prospects and the ramifications of war force first-hand awareness (likely for a couple of generations) of the spiritual and economic debilitation that comes with war.

106. General Thoughts on War and Peace.

- Altruism is not born of and is always interrupted by reality.
- The war for power is never at peace.
- Lawlessness breeds authoritarianism which breeds new lawlessness.
- Peace is evident in those who are at peace, even in times of war.
- Inner peace based on external stimuli is neither inner nor peaceful.
- Violence is the result of conflicting excesses.
- Economic and social sustainability, while interdependent, are always in conflict.
- Cycles of war and peace often repeat with more than an echo.
- War can be a future deterrent to war if generations teach the consequences of war.
- Nation states fund militaries to keep the peace but finances are insufficient to keep foreign peace.

107. Value Free Choice If You Want to Keep It.

Free choices are the means for creating economic and spiritual advantage. Choices enable us to optimize profit, to be cost efficient, and to be different in kind and in degree. When we permit or are forced to permit others to dictate our choices or to make choices for us in return for security, we lose our free choices, first one and then another. Similarly, standing by when others lose their free choices without speaking up puts us next in line to lose our freedom to choose. Freedoms must be guarded with urgency, no matter how minor the threat. Those who undervalue free choice and the power derived therefrom end up with no choice.

History is replete with examples, teaching that freedom has never been free, never lasted, and never fully valued. The fight for free choice is one that each generation must wage. The more value each generation ascribes to freedom, the more the next generation will embrace the fight for freedom. The more distracted a generation regarding individual freedoms, the more likely those freedoms will be lost by the present generation or the next.

108. Capitalism Critics Are Unaware That Profit Must Fuel an Engine.

Capitalism at work is the best economic system yet devised by man. It incentivizes new creations every day while deconstructing the old and less efficient. A new creation does not have to be totally new, just new enough to be more efficient, more dependable, and more profitable than current creations. Those who criticize change, in whatever form, own part of the status quo, if in mind only. Warnings of obsolescence fall on deaf ears until they are real to those who are obsolete or are becoming obsolete. When disfunction comes, critics focus blame on leaders who should have seen that end coming rather than focusing on new opportunities. But the real problem is always that few are willing to listen, see, and comprehend in advance.

Capitalism does run in cycles. There are times of investment in "new" and times of disinvestment because the once "new" has become old and exhausted. Too much of the same things become available in copycat fashion. Peaks in the investment cycle can lead to an exhausted, dispossessed, and hurting population, looking to socialism, communism, and dictators for new directions and not willing to wait for consolidation and rebuilding. Attitude, individual and collective, is everything in economics.

Many nations like today's Venezuela and yesterday's Cuba voted in socialism, not realizing that socialism has never been viable for more than the time it takes to raid public and private wealth. After monies have been expropriated from the rich and the less than rich, all loose purchasing power, jobs, and resources. Food and essentials become scarce. Redistribution of wealth drains an economy and fosters increasing corruption.

109. Obesity Kills Bodies and Corporate Bodies.

Obesity is both a condition and a disease. Too much fat is not healthy, but few really know how much fat will cause vital functions to fail. Medications alleviate symptoms, but diet and exercise are keys to core health in bodies and economics.

Businesses and governments are much the same. Too much fat, too rich a spending diet, and too little efficiency creates a spending problem. Borrowing money can cure a cash flow problem temporarily; however, earnings are the best budgeting control solution. Outside investors can be brought in, but new money lasts only if earnings exceed spending.

The founders of the United States Constitution presumed that collective heads would control spending. Obviously, with $21 plus trillion to $200 plus trillion in debt (depending on what is included), that assumption is not working. One alternative to continued mis-management is a constitutional amendment to limit governmental spending, but that has faced a tough road given the vested interests who benefit from spending. For perspective, a no-deduction 10 percent tax could fund the vitals; a 15 percent tax rate could fund the vitals plus some social programs; a 20 percent tax rate endangers the nation. Politicians succumb to the temptation to promise more spending to garner votes and solidify too long a place in the halls of congress for themselves and the bureaucracy. Federal and state governments have followed suit on their way to obesity. Free food tends to promote obesity; meanwhile, parasites become obese on free food.

110. Be Aware of the Real, the Unreal, and the Surreal.

Real is fact, true, actual, operational, and not imaginary. Unreal is false and untenable. Surreal can be defined as an irrational or wishful arrangement of material, facts, and/or opinions. Everyone exists in the real but may embrace the unreal or the surreal for purposeful gain, comfort, temporary security, fantasy, or just plain unawareness. The unreal never lasts but may be sustained for a time by surreal agents. Situations often contain all three, which change and, at some point, trend toward true reality.

The Powers That Be (TPTB) want their minions to believe in a reality that suits TPTB purposes. TPTB frantically try to correct their errors by proffering a new best way to govern, spend, and lead. They message their new way while hiding their own faults by promoting the unreal and the surreal when the real is not currently palatable. TPTB dispute or destroy options while messaging us that the king's new suit of clothes is not nakedness.

Reality has its own way of appearing when needed. Seasons of lies end when the fragility of overhyped systemic promises cannot be kept, money supplies dwindle, and a politic is unsustainable. Distinguishing between the real, the unreal, and the surreal is almost a full-time job when reporting clings to the unreal and the surreal almost wistfully. Agendas become more important than truth, and information is skewed to suit. As confusion and unrest grow, reality peers through the cracks. When more people realize the falsity of it all, they learn that real economics trump the politics of TPTB every time in its appointed time.

111. The Soul of a Nation Operates on Faith.

- Faith in the rule of law must be important to more than a citizen majority.
- Complexity requires faith beyond experience to operate consistently.
- Empires rise and fall when a populace loses faith in promises made.
- Nations and individuals thrive if souls remain faithful to reason and responsibility.
- Faithful commitment and work build the foundation of a nation.
- Opinion must be faithful to truth if opinion is to matter.
- Uniting in crises requires the souls of people to have faith in more than self-interest.
- Faithful leaders do not create or spread confusion.
- Paganism from within is more threatening to a nation's soul than paganism from without.
- The soul of a nation breathes only if God is honored.

112. Black Swan Events Happen, Ready or Not.

Clear sailing should not be assumed in any sea. In calm seas, we become linear thinkers, seeking safe passage and forgetting that unseen storms always meet us on their terms. We dismiss the idea that order and disorder follow one another in a never-ending struggle and that every person's life is disrupted to one degree or another multiple times. We rely on what we know for stability and tend to want to know that which we already know.

Black swan events may startle one alone, or they may wake up entire societies. They may be short-term and localized or game changers for nations and all time. Unexpected (sometimes catastrophic) things happen in curious times; often, when we fail to recognize the times.

Not every black swan event is a sign of pending doom. Yet, there is an unease that falls on those affected by their black swan. Fear and confusion are characteristic responses. But prior to most black swan events, a certain foreboding comes upon the situationally aware.

When background noise increases at an increasing rate, people wonder, but not everyone is motivated by their sense of foreboding. Noah, on the other hand, spent approximately 100 years building an ark for a laughable purpose until the rains began to fall.

Cycles in sun activity, earthquakes, financial panics, and war all portend change. Uncertainty produces fear which can produce opposite responses: chaos or preparedness. Fear may motivate the preparedness, but fear, by itself, accomplishes little. Organizing a response to potential dangers accomplishes a lot if families, neighborhoods, and nations reason together and act together to mitigate or survive a threat.

Different situations warrant organizing differently, but all things work for good when God is primal in the organizing. The following list of ideas speak to secondary human basics of being ready in time and for all times:

- Most black swan events possess a history that forecast potential occurrences.

- Wealthy people often "rent" to be ready and adroit for changes in fundamental economics.
- Locked, loaded, and knowing when and how to defend is readiness in harm's way.
- Freeze-dried food is not gourmet, but gourmet matters little to hungry stomachs.
- Water is the most needed and a most-taken-for-granted asset in civilized societies.
- "Ready" implies knowledge which requires effort.
- A sensitive heart is more prepared than a hardhead.
- Self-control is a vital part of readiness.
- Man's nature is to be part of a crisis before responding to the crisis.
- Governments hide crises until populations are significantly affected.

113. God Often Replaces Comfort with Discomfort for Good Purpose.

Man's free will and God's will are undependably linked. We cannot predict outcomes, but with God at our side, we can be at peace with whatever comes and usually learn more from discomfort than comfort. Since good and evil are always at enmity, we learn that peace must be interrupted to maintain the best peace. In the process, we often find that what we sought turns out to be less than something better.

114. The Economics of Power Are Counterintuitive.

Power is a wasting asset; it depreciates over time. Dictators, military leaders, anarchists, the wealthy, church hierarchies, and others on the rise use and grow power in every means possible. Power seekers usurp what the already powerful possess for there is only so much power to go around, learning quickly that power generates its own economics. Those who grab hold can hold on only for so long.

Power has a unique way of working internally against those in power. The more power one possesses, the more the internal conflict. Anger, deceit, ego, paranoia, lust, and a host of other sins creep in. Like drug addicts, the quest for power may begin small and with good purpose. However, prolonged power breeds dependence, self-absorption, protectionism, and gaming provider systems. Boasting becomes a habit, and the boasting is not about strength that lasts.

Power does not have to end in wickedness. Those who use power for good grow to become worthy of more. Those in power who get on their knees every day before the Lord gain unexpected wisdom. Those who see power as a force to be used for others often gain the respect of others. Power used for eternal purposes is power never wasted.

Note: Power is not limited to leaders of nations; its use applies to all who hold power over one or many.

115. The Situation with Government Finances Is Always in Doubt.

Governments promise most everything, deliver most everything poorly, and take every advantage of the rich and poor to keep doing everything poorly, including promising. To be fair, the more wants a population wants, the more that population thinks others should want to provide, often with government assistance. To be accurate, government largesse is as much about personal gain as social benefit.

Governments do not produce economic wealth but live to transfer it. Like anything in man's economy, government consumption can become addictive. Feeding the beast to the point of addiction leads to a bigger beast with a bigger appetite.

Greater tax revenues for governments hold the answer for every obscure purpose under heaven. Unfortunately, the spenders do not see the opportunity cost lost when those who created wealth are forced to pay taxes and fees in lieu of further wealth creation. The least cost to all and the greatest gain for all lies in what is missing: the freedom to invoke the *Invisible Hand*. Spending someone else's money should be left to that someone else.

116. Reasons Why America's Present Systems Are Obsolete.

- The efficiency of U.S. institutions has devolved over time, financially and functionally.
- National, state, and municipal government debt cannot be repaid.
- Adam Smith's *Invisible Hand* has been shackled by political and economic socialism.
- Social programs that promote idleness promote bankruptcy.
- Foreign expeditions have cost more than they profited.
- Multiculturalism is an idol that inherently destroys cohesion and common purpose.
- Computers and devices have replaced critical thought and action.
- Life essentials are unaffordable for many, if not most.
- Misinformation and disinformation abound in the public square.
- "Legal" has become a matter of power, influence, and corruption and more than expensive.
- Dependability and accountability are not taught, modelled, or implemented.
- Institutional "swamps" spend mightily to protect and promote themselves.
- The U.S. Constitution faces wrecking crews hired by special interests seeking advantage.
- The highest and best use of present human systems is deconstruction and building anew.

117. Be Aware of the Prospects for Collapse.

Collapses are sudden, unexpected, and often consequential. Collapses destroy our faith in the health and well-being of institutions and governments. When collapse happens, the first step to saving the world is saving ourselves from ourselves. Fear and panic often accompany collapse, especially when the fragility of human delivery systems become personal. The larger the system, the more likely the effects of collapse will spread to other systems. Equity markets, banking systems, pension funds, international trade, and currency partners are not immune. Solvency of each is the end game with each trying to protect its own turf.

Theories of collapse mean little until the collapse is felt directly. For decades, short-term economics have weakened long-term financial foundations across the economic world. Bandages are no longer sufficient for deep wounds. Healing will require surgery, cleansing antiseptics, antibiotics, staples, and more. Pain is coming. Your faith will be tested. The best antidote is prayer, but pray not for less pain; pray for understanding, providence, and resolve.

118. Missing Seven Meals Changes Personal Economics.

So much is taken for granted by those who have enough and even those who do not. Freedom, food, family, and finances (the 4Fs) are change initiators when interrupted. Take just one away and things look markedly different. For example, missing seven meals in a row is a game changer. That creates a hunger and a wonder for the eighth meal and beyond. The resulting insecurity begins to challenge basic assumptions, even those of civility. Formerly unnecessary, foraging for absolute necessities for self and family must be learned on the job. Spread across a whole society, the economics of everything else become secondary to the economics of water, food, shelter, and survival.

Affluence leads to wistful demands that "government should provide," "we should be free to choose," "hurt feelings are most important," "I deserve," "organic is necessary," or "love everyone" be met. But past affluence is no remedy for emerging shortages in vital essentials. Fasting is a choice while starvation is a matter of life and death. Missing seven meals places opinion, emotion, and wistful demands in perspective. Action cannot wait. Survival skill sets become necessary and sought. The world of personal economics is just as critical as it always has been, but we have assumed (for too long) that someone else would take care of the "critical" for us. Know that help may not be on its way, but no matter the way, you can help.

119. Can You Bank on Your Bank?

Bank managements have a fiduciary duty to make money for their stockholders first and foremost. Depositors deposit money to earn interest or to take advantage of bank payments and credit card systems while banks theoretically lend some of those deposits to creditworthy borrowers who pay interest and fees to the bank. Bank managements know that their profits and the bank deposits are only as safe as borrower repayments and transaction reimbursements from other banks. But the solvency of the financial system itself may be an equal cause of concern.

Government steps in to regulate, audit, and provide certain guarantees of solvency for member banks. Solvency of the banking system and member banks is never constant and not to be assumed. You can assume, however, that you will not be first in line if a credit crisis hits. You can also assume that bank management will put their personal and bank safety first and foremost. If banks begin to lose confidence in the routine of being paid amounts owed by other banks, banking liquidity dries up. Be more than aware that the Federal Deposit Insurance Corporation does not have enough money (unless the treasury prints money out of thin air) to handle even a small systemic crisis. Your best insurance may be keeping your money and valuables, or some portion thereof, outside the banking system.

120. How Long Would/Should/Could You Feed Hungry Neighbors?

The Great Depression is famous for its long bread lines. The popular view is that it could never happen again in America. An unnoticed view is that for many recent decades, we have processed longer food lines than seen in the 1930s stark photos, using EBT cards, welfare checks, subsidized housing, and many other forms of assistance. In fact, well over 50 percent of Americans (and some foreign nationals) receive some form of government subsidy. Should we or can we keep free money flowing? Should or can we limit subsidies? We all know what is popular and with whom.

Government debt burdens more than suggest that our limits have been reached. Big help from big government is nearing an end. Necessary help may then become a local matter and on a smaller scale. The greater the need for help, the greater the potential disappointment and resulting chaos. The greater the chaos, the greater the focus on those near and dear. Self-preservation forces family and friends to pull together to meet needs. Resources determine how many can be included. The question for each group (and person within that group) is how far to extend available resources to those outside the group. The less you have, the more you will want and the more you need and the less likely you will find it as others compete for scarce supplies. Moral and economic questions arise quickly in chaos, leading to moral and economic dilemmas. There is no perfect answer. Groups will decide differently. The choice of who and what to share is never easy in situational chaos. Unfortunately, the reality is that there will not be enough stores/caches/inventories to accommodate the needs.

121. Have You Contemplated the Need to Contemplate the End-Times?

History has no record of previous *end-times* simply because mankind has never faced the end-times. With little specifics to go on, few contemplate what may lie ahead or when it will come. The Bible speaks to the Second Coming of Christ and events which precede such a miraculous happening. Times of tribulation and turning from God set the stage. An antichrist, leading a world government and an unknowing population, slyly turns all but a remnant of believers away from God. Many believers face persecution. Large numbers of the world population cease to exist. Chaos reigns, courtesy of Satan's legacy and direction.

One alarming contemplation centers on what would happen if God removes His *Invisible Hand* of protection from our civilization. Those who were building the Tower of Babel, those living in the times of Noah, and those witnessing the fall of the Roman Empire offer one bit of advice. Foresight is better than hindsight. Ask yourself what risks face you today. Then ask yourself if these times are simply a systemic end to times that you have known or the *end-times*. Whether you think the end-times are coming soon or not, always be prepared spiritually.

122. Coming Back from the Brink.

In financial terms, we are on the brink of a tumultuous credit bubble bursting. Debt is unsustainable, unrepayable, and unaffordable among sovereign governments, public and private institutions, and at home. Rainy-day stores are depleted.

Gloom on the horizon is not a subject to trifle with nor is it a matter for fright. Despite the likelihood that, in our present situation, there is no turning back, no reset button, and no easy solution, fear does not bring one or many back safely from the brink. Frantically rearranging the deck chairs on a sinking Titanic is not constructive. The will and the courage to face reality is. On a personal level, the time to prepare is now. Dependence on sovereigns is not a viable long-term option any longer.

Nationalist movements around the globe should tell us that one world government is losing favor because of false premises and promises. Federal and state government debts should forewarn us to look to local solutions; however, local governments have caught the same debt disease, warning that desires and many needs cannot be sustained.

We face statistical no man's land. We are entering a "left tail" risk situation which is more than three standard deviations removed from the mean in a negative direction. That far removed from normal means that anything is possible. But take heart, the negative can lead to positive after deconstruction is complete. Opportunities will abound for replacing that which existed but failed.

There is very little that we have come to value that will hold its value. Essentials like food, water, medicine, and energy always hold their value but will likely become scarce and expensive. It is a time to think ahead, about what will exist in the deconstruction and rebuilding process. God-fearing leaders must be raised up.

As with everything, God is in control. But God cannot be happy with our turning away from Him and His mandates. If enough turn back to Him and soon, some consequences may be mitigated. However, many empires, even those once established under God, have fallen due to misguided spiritual and economic adventures. Fallen is not always a bad thing if it drives us back to God. Standing on a rock is always preferable to the shifting sands we have ventured toward for too long.

123. Trust in the Lord in the Best and Worst Situations.

Keeping life simple is far from of being a simpleton. Those who prefer the supposed sophistication of their "own understanding" lose sight of the basic economics of life, the straight versus the crooked paths to success and failure, the benefits of avoiding evil and its produce, and the serenity found in the Lord's admonitions. A few bits of practical wisdom go a long way.

124. Specific Warnings and Admonitions for the World Situation.

Situational Awareness is about recognition, wisdom, and action. The three operate jointly to maximize the "best" and minimize the "worst" in people and pending economics of life. Both maximizing and minimizing require an awareness beyond the obvious, a sense of historical perspective, a recognition of the carnal nature of mankind, and an acceptance that generally accepted solutions may not suffice.

Eternal situational awareness embraces the fact that walking with the *Invisible Hand* of God is a lifetime pursuit. Those who love the Lord need not worry about the world regardless of condition, for the Lord is in the heavens and salvation is assured. His promise that nothing will separate us from His love and His plans for believers is assured.

Creation awareness for our times leads us to consider the times of Noah and the debauchery of mankind that led to the great flood and to consider the times of the Tower of Babel and man's haughty notion that he and she could be like God. In Noah's time, complete destruction occurred. In Babel, people were dispersed, their construction project was never completed, their spoken languages were unrecognizable one to another, and their common objectives in life no longer remained common. Death, destruction, disaffectedness, and dispute (the 4Ds) are key indicators of a world gone mad apart from God.

The following lists of *warnings and admonitions* are intended to give you a glimpse into what could happen. Of course, and hopefully, God can step in to ease our pain at any time in any manner, according to His good pleasure. Believers and nonbelievers will not likely be spared trials and tribulations resulting from past individual and societal choices and behaviors.

Before reading the list containing warnings and admonitions, please take a moment to ask God to reveal what truths are important and which of this author's imaginings are not. Ask Him to comfort you as you plan, to protect you as you act, and to reveal to you what you should and should not do for or with others. The intent here is not to unduly alarm you nor to worry you beyond that which the Lord would use to awaken you. History suggests that the world will not end tomorrow, but, if it does, the Lord has promised a regal place in Heaven for believers.

Being prepared as God would lead is never a wasting proposition. Ask Joseph about preparedness. Think of Noah building an ark and being ridiculed by those who were blind to the times. Today's challenges likely fit in between the Joseph and Noah situations, unless the *end-times* are upon us. The *Spiritual Awareness, Life Economics Awareness* and *Macroeconomic and Geopolitical Awareness* posited in this book provide but a simple foundation upon which to build the future and what it may come to be.

125. Economic and Spiritual Warnings in a World Gone Mad.

- Many public and private pension plan schemes will likely perform negatively in real money terms and may be underwater now.
- Bank closures and forced financial mergers may become commonplace, placing deposits at risk.
- Attacks on Christianity will increase with opponents turning to restrictions or violence.
- Economic reset strategies will increase with decreasing results.
- Economic necessities will trump social/political correctness in government and in the streets.
- False doctrines, false prophets, and false churches will try to deceive the masses one by one.
- The bigger the number of moving parts in your life, the harder it will be to control.
- Irrational exuberance will continue to a breaking point.
- Most debt/derivatives cannot be repaid which will severely hurt lenders and those they owe.
- Fiat currencies hold only speculative values and for shortening periods.
- Depopulation is likely and in massive numbers as economic destruction and war rage.
- Separationist movements will infect countries and states within states.
- College debt in the trillions is unsustainable for lenders and borrowers with consequences.
- The cycle of war and rumors of wars will be seen and heard as governments seek resources.
- Governments will be increasingly able to do less for dependents.
- Just-in-time delivery systems may fracture, creating shortage and panic.
- Residents and nonresidents will experience adversity from bankrupt states.

- A declining petrodollar will create new bank payment networks and mediums of exchange.
- Those in urban areas will find family, freedoms and finances in jeopardy first.
- Expect to be asked for more by friends who once took necessities for granted.
- No country will be immune from resource wars.
- A Convention of States may be the only way to preserve the United States.
- Beware of misinformation campaigns that steer sheeple into preferred pastures.
- Military tribunals will be employed against the treasonous.
- States with the most debt will enact the most restrictions. Move if you should.
- Declining purchasing power leads to fewer dependable sellers with less inventory.
- Patriots will be targeted by those in power as enemies.
- Massive sunspots, earthquakes, hurricanes, etc. repeat in cycles as does awareness.
- The United States Constitution gives the freedom to be responsible but not irresponsible and it will be tested.
- The skewed economic statistics you have been fed are not worth eating.
- The economically, technologically, or militarily weak are the first to succumb.
- Tangible assets are most tangible when needed and most demanded when intangibles deflate.
- When a government is forced to purchase its own debt, that debt is hidden until worthless.
- Anarchists know that destroying the middle class is the sure way to destroy a nation.
- Whole life insurance policies will be paid out in worthless currency if the insurer survives.
- Medicine shortages will occur from a lack of money to manufacture, distribute, and purchase.
- Confidence in systems will decrease at an increasing rate.

- As more debt is required to create the next unit of production, the population will see that government policies do not know economics.
- Gold and silver coins have historically been currency and will be again.
- Education will be forced by economics to go back to the basics in simpler places.
- Low interest rates artificially reduce government expense, incentivize spending, and hurt savers while jeopardizing the solvency of pensions and other fixed income investments.
- Local real estate and income taxes will be levied with little concern about its affordability.
- Off-balance sheet debt and unfunded liabilities tell the real story about U.S. Treasury solvency.
- Venezuela proves that giving up personal freedom for economic security is not secure for long.
- Empires fall greatest when there is laughter at the prospects for their demise.
- Neither heads in the sand nor rose-colored glasses change real economics or war.
- Sharia law and fascism grow from the same seed planted by men to control all men.
- Will an impersonal government care about you when those in power are at risk?
- The world cares about the United States only as far as the largesse provided.
- Acts of cyber war may interrupt or destroy power grids, water treatment, business supply chains, government services, and much we depend on.
- Skilled doctors, nurses, EMTs, etc. may want to be anonymous in a full-blown crisis.
- Electromagnetic pulses can destroy heating, transport, communications, and most electronics.
- There was only so much room in Noah's ark and only one ark builder.
- Preparedness may be labeled quirky and unpatriotic by ruling bureaucracies.

126. A Potpourri of Spiritual and Preparedness Admonitions Midst the Madness.

- Christ never told believers to love the sin equal to the sinner as secularists and sinners claim.
- Use the internet to see if your bank passed its latest financial stress test.
- Contentment in God does not justify complacency in man.
- Stewardship is taking care of the ship and crew in calm and rough seas.
- Prepare for war with those who seek to be at war with you for wrong reasons.
- Local churches may not be like-minded in preparedness urgency, except for the Mormons.
- Ask local law enforcement and military friends how long they would choose government over citizens.
- Those who have helped Israel receive blessings, those against Israel will not.
- Store food and water for those dear to you for six months, plus a 10 percent discretionary tithe.
- Organize like-minded people with disparate skill sets within your family and neighborhood.
- Own gold, silver and lead and other tangibles while you can and keep them close.
- Growing food and knowing how to protect that food are skills to acquire now.
- Be more than on guard for desperate neighbors and rovers in need.
- Prepare for life without electricity and all that it powers.
- Needed health care procedures and prescriptions should be acquired now.
- Some cash at home may be safer than cash in the bank.
- Plan for alternate means of communication before a telecommunications blackout.
- High gas mileage vehicles are an asset, especially when little fuel is available.

- Preaching the Good News of Salvation is apt for all times and all situations.
- Pray for wisdom every day in every way for yourself and others.
- Heirloom seeds can produce new seeds but genetically modified seeds do not.
- Locate more alternative water sources than you think necessary.
- Ammunition runs out quickly, especially if you need it.
- A second passport and a legal offshore account may be part of plan B for some.
- Never become weary of doing good for good possesses the greatest value in chaos.
- Spare parts, batteries, tires, tools, radios, screws, etc. may not always be accessible.
- Locate a safe place with friends, stock it and keep it known only to the group.
- Know the gods you worship, the returns they bring, and the disorder they create.
- Giving thanks for what we have changes the focus from what we do or may not have.
- Reality may change, but additional talents and training help change reality.
- Chaos creates a new reality for kids; adults can help them cope with their fears and direction.
- Be meek whether leading or following, aware that meek is not weak.
- Look to old power generators for simplicity, repair ability, and multiple fuel options.
- Power water systems first, food storage next, heating next; cooling is a luxury.
- Research drinking water standards and create ways to meet them from sources not on tap.
- HAM radio licenses/knowledge/equipment may be essential in crisis, locally and regionally.

- Bible reading neighborhoods/states are better founded and grounded when survival is at issue.
- Night vision goggles/scopes provide an edge on offense and a great equalizer on defense.
- Do not expect to save those who are lukewarm about their commitment to help save others.
- Redundancy is always costly, often needed, and never completely adequate for the unknown.
- Know how to use guns safely; also, know that guns do not work long without spare parts.
- Underground storage at fifty-five dry degrees preserves most everything at the least cost.
- Solar panels have become generic; the connected batteries determine long-term efficiency.
- Antiseptics and antibiotics are vital to life. Store some and rotate as needed.
- Remember the Sabbath Day and remember its application each day in comfort and crisis.

Marching Orders

We have transitioned in this book from identifying the underlying economics in God's creation to the spiritual and attitudinal factors that influence day-to-day thoughts and actions. Finally, we have described the macroeconomic and geopolitical situation in which we find ourselves today. We can now better see that everything spiritual, economic and geopolitical is part of a whole. The whole, and your part in it today, is either viable or not.

This author is not a financial advisor, nor is specific financial advice to be implied. Seek your own trusted financial expert for matters of this material world but rely on God for spiritual guidance and life economic investments. Every day for you is different than any other day and every life is its own unique situation. Every day of every life is filled with @Risk situations that require more faithfulness than most people possess.

Every generation is responsible for societal, political and economic cycles. War and peace, boom and bust, health and plagues, calm and storms, and turning to and from God are part of the ongoing human condition. Therefore, please view each Warning as possible. Please consider each admonition as something to be addressed with a conscious commitment.

Know that we cannot be prepared for every event. We should not even try, for in the attempt, we may create an untenable idol and accompanying phobias. Know too, that as we hold on to our present, our future is unfolding, whether we seek it or even see it, or not. A host of unknowns always plague our understanding. They are to be faced, not feared. Detours are to be embraced with God at the helm. Use Joseph's preparation skills when black swans appear on the horizon; see them early and remember that lifeboats are always nice to have on hand.

Whatever our condition, God has given us commandments and admonitions with which to act. They work! But disobeying them ends poorly. God's rules of order counterbalance the @Risk disorder that we create. *The Invisible Hand* is with us to guide us, prompting us to seek God in every matter, to seek real profit, both spiritual and economic, for more than just ourselves in every opportunity. Importantly, we are to be guardians of His truth in all that we say or do.

I pray that the topics herein are presented fairly and that the recommended mindsets are in keeping with God's ordained righteousness, order and honor. To guard against this author's error in the writings contained herein, call on the Lord and He will answer you. He has promised to show you "great and mighty things." Whatever you need to know, you will come to know, if you ask God and pursue your own situational awareness and considered responses. Always try to add substance where substance is missing, and the world will be a better place.

Be of good courage in each personal, economic and macro situation! Do not tremble or be dismayed, for the Lord is with you and He will lead. Be more than aware of eternal priorities midst earthly chaos. Do not allow the times and seasons of life to define you. Be bold, be active and be committed. Never forget the transformational power of love. Change the world for the better from wherever you begin. Lead those who will follow you or follow those who would lead you in the Lord's direction and begin now. May the Lord bless you and keep you!

Awareness Topical Index

III. Macroeconomic and Political Awareness: The Proximate and the Remote Are Intertwined for Better and for Worse—Yesterday, Today and Tomorrow 109

About the Author

Gordon Brown has been blessed with a good education, a healthy family, a wealth of business experiences, and enough trials and tribulations along the way to gain certain life perspectives in keeping with God's holy word. He maintains that he learned all too quickly that his PhD degree did not guarantee wisdom for that is a lifelong quest. The author's many patents, business successes and failures, college teaching, and social and political endeavors have taught Gordon how important knowing what to do, how to do it, and when to act varies with each situation. Many of his greatest lessons were learned in the hard times rather than those of comfort and security.

Friends and colleagues, eight children and twenty-one grandchildren have proven to him that everyone sees life through multiple prisms. The author's many journal articles focused on a specific subject, but the subject of life and the economics of life require more than one view, one decision, and one action. Gordon has a preoccupation with awareness of more than his own interpretations and, in particular, God's hand in the world and in each life story. The more aware a person is of self and more than self, the more productive the life.

CPSIA information can be obtained
at www.ICGtesting.com
Printed in the USA
LVHW090155051019
633263LV00001B/14/P

9 781645 591849